DIRT SIMPLE FIDDLE

BY
MARY ANN WILLIS

www.melbay.com/21381BCDEB

Audio Contents

1 Tuning the G String
2 Tuning the D String
3 Tuning the A String
4 Tuning the E String
5 Sawstroke on the Open Strings
6 Hot Cross Buns
7 Shuffle Bowing
8 Boil the Cabbage Down
9 Boil the Cabbage Down with Drones
10 Boil the Cabbage Down on the A String
11 Boil the Cabbage Down on the Top Two Strings
12 Mary Had a Little Lamb
13 Angeline the Baker
14 Cripple Creek
15 Cripple Creek with Shuffle Bowing and Drones
16 Cripple Creek with Slides
17 Cripple Creek Intro
18 Cripple Creek with Everything
19 McNab's Hornpipe - Dipping the Bow
20 McNab's Hornpipe - Rocking the Bow
21 Liza Jane
22 Liza Jane - Fancy Version
23 Old Joe Clark
24 Old Joe Clark with Hammer-ons and Pull-offs
25 Old Joe Clark with Shuffle Bowing and Drones
26 Red-Haired Boy
27 Pop! Goes the Weasel
28 Soldier's Joy
29 Soldier's Joy with 1-and-3 Bowing
30 Soldier's Joy with Progressing Lines
31 Devil's Dream
32 Devil's Dream Tag
33 Arkansas Traveler
34 St. Anne's Reel
35 Turkey in the Straw
36 Log Chain
37 Battle of New Orleans
38 Tennessee Waltz
39 Rubber Dolly
40 B with Cross-Shuffle
41 B with Alternating Top Notes
42 B with Progressing Top Notes
43 Random Rag
44 Sally Goodin
45 Billy in the Lowground
46 Liberty
47 I Don't Love Nobody
48 Demo

Credits

Brady Lanier, Rebecca Oswald - engraving *Bede Van Dyke - graphics*

Dan Lewis, Bede Van Dyke, Rebecca Oswald - photography

David Noll - audio engineering and guitar *Mary Ann Willis - violin*

http://www.youtube.com/dirtsimplefiddle

WWW.MELBAY.COM

Table of Contents

Parts of the Fiddle and Bow 3
Tune the Fiddle 4
Accessories 4
Tighten the Bow Hair 6
Rosin the Bow 6
Holding the Fiddle 7
Holding the Bow 8
To Make a Good Sound 8
The Open Strings....................................9
Sawstroke on the Open Strings 10
Loosen the Bow Hair 10
Note Names 11
Note Durations 11
Reading Music 12
Notes on the A String 14
Accurate Intonation 14
Left Hand Position 15
Hot Cross Buns!....................................16
Shuffle Bowing 17
Boil the Cabbage Down 18
Boil the Cabbage Down with Drones 19
Boil the Cabbage Down on the A String 20
Boil the Cabbage Down on the Top Two Strings 21
Mary Had a Little Lamb 22
Angeline the Baker 23
Cripple Creek 24
Cripple Creek with Shuffle Bowing and Drones..25
Cripple Creek with Slides 27
Cripple Creek Intro 27
McNab's Hornpipe - Dipping the Bow 28
McNab's Hornpipe - Rocking the Bow....................................29
Liza Jane 30
Liza Jane Fancy Version 30
Old Joe Clark 31
Old Joe Clark with Hammer-ons and Pull-offs ..32
Old Joe Clark with Shuffle Bowing and Drones 34
Red-Haired Boy 35
Pop! Goes the Weasel 36
Soldier's Joy 36
Soldier's Joy with 1-and-3 Bowing 38
Soldier's Joy with Progressing Lines 39
Devil's Dream 40
Devil's Dream Tag....................................41
Arkansas Traveler 42
St. Anne's Reel 43
Turkey in the Straw 44
Log Chain 45
Battle of New Orleans 46
Tennessee Waltz 47
Rubber Dolly 48
Rubber Dolly Alternate [B] with Cross-Shuffle 49
Rubber Dolly Alternate [B] with Alternating Top Note Cross-Shuffle 50
Rubber Dolly Alternate [B] with Progressing Top Note Cross-Shuffle....................................51
Random Rag 52
Sally Goodin....................................53
Billy in the Lowground 54
Liberty 55
I Don't Love Nobody 56
About the Author 57
Practice Tips 58
Notes on the Fiddle 59
Alphabetical Index of Tunes 60

PARTS of the FIDDLE and BOW

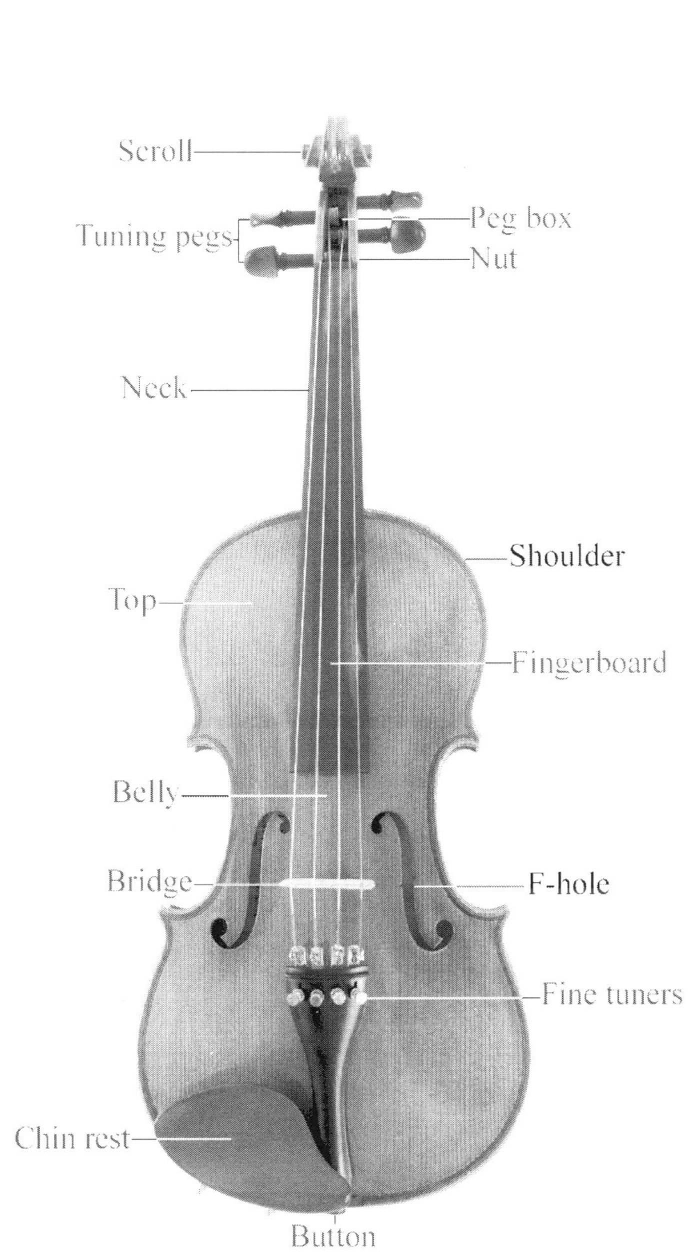

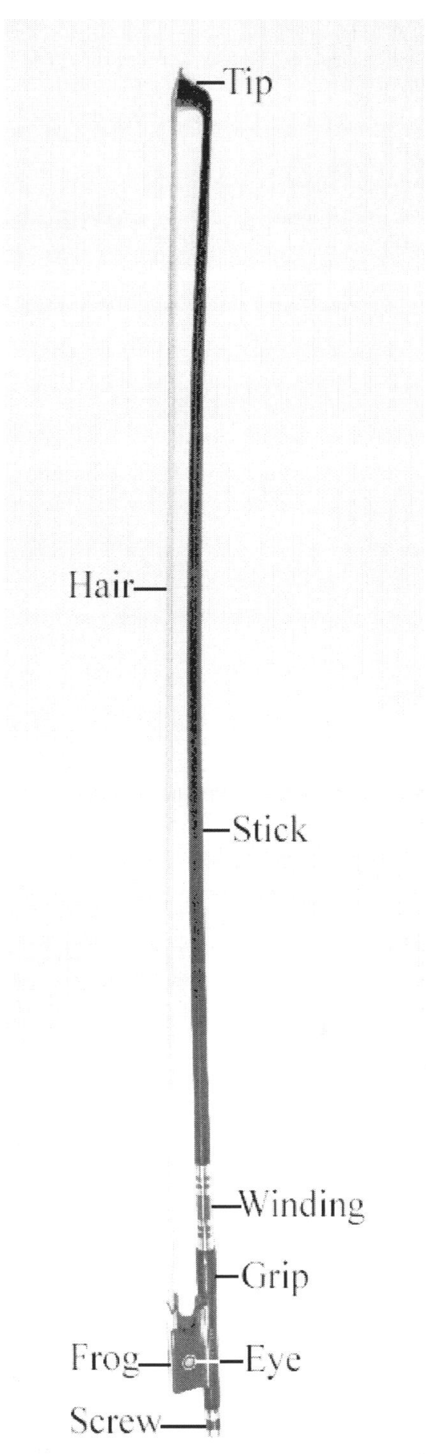

KEEP YOUR FIDDLE AT A COMFORTABLE TEMPERATURE AND HUMIDITY AND IT WILL REPAY YOU WITH YEARS OF GOOD SERVICE.

ACCESSORIES

Shoulder rest - helps you hold the fiddle up.

Rosin - makes the bow hair grip the string to produce a sound.

Spare strings - you never know when one will break!

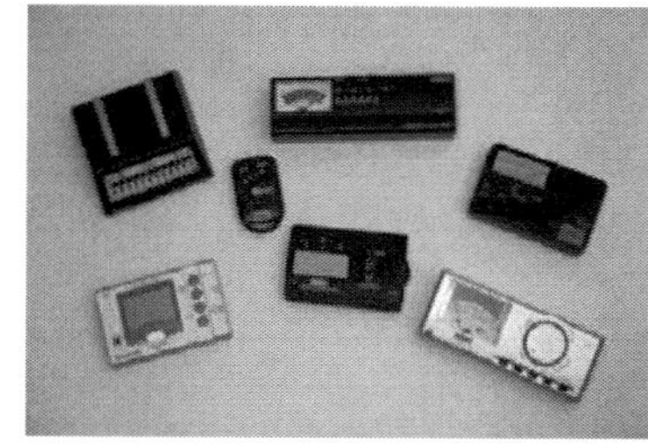

Tuner - or you can find a virtual one online.

TUNE the FIDDLE

String Names

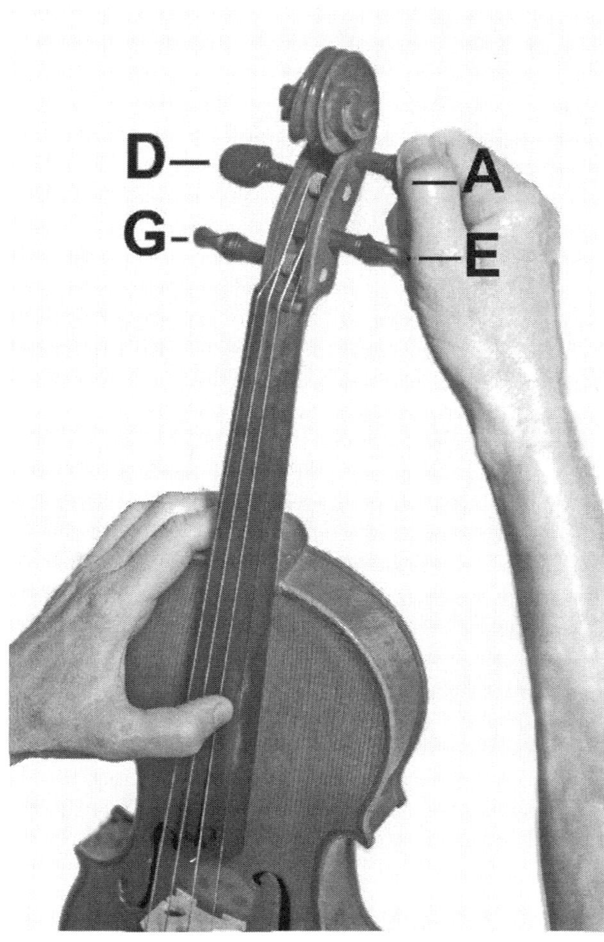

Use the tuning track on the companion recording, or a tuner.

- Hold the fiddle upright on your lap (facing you).
- Hold it by the shoulder as shown.
- Always loosen the string first. That way, if you're accidentally trying to tune a different string from the one you're plucking, it won't break.
- Pluck the string repeatedly with your thumb as you tune it.
- Turn the peg toward you to lower the pitch, then away from you to raise it.
- Push the peg in enough while you turn it to make it grip.

Avoid plucking in the bow path. Finger oils can make it slick.

- Use the fine tuner to finish the job; turn its head counterclockwise to lower the pitch; clockwise to raise it.
- Tune the E string with the fine tuner only, unless it's way out of tune.
- Go back and re-check all four strings.

(When your tuners get tightened down almost all the way, back them off and re-tune with the pegs. Make sure they're not digging into the top of the fiddle!)

BEFORE PLAYING

Tighten the bow hair:

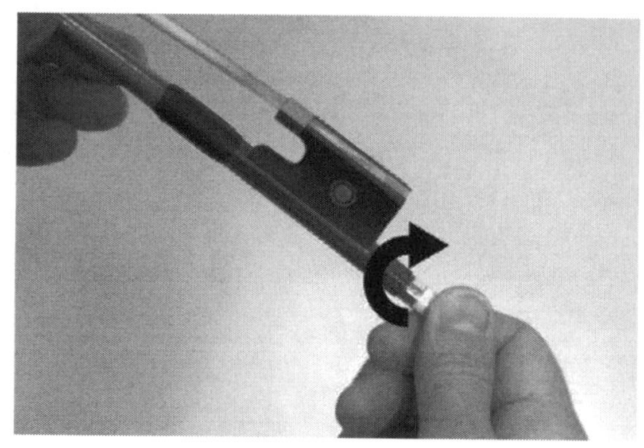

If the hair is touching the stick, tighten it, to keep the stick from scraping the string.

- Turn the screw clockwise.

CAUTION! Avoid touching the playing surface of the hair.
Finger oils can make it slick.

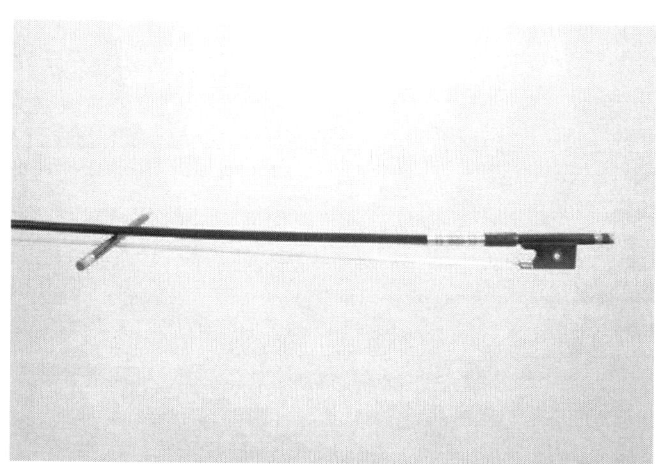

- Turn the screw until the space between the hair and the stick (at the middle) is about as wide as a pencil.
- If the bow hair touches the stick when you play, tighten it some more.
- If the bow bounces uncontrollably when you play, loosen the hair.

Rosin the bow:

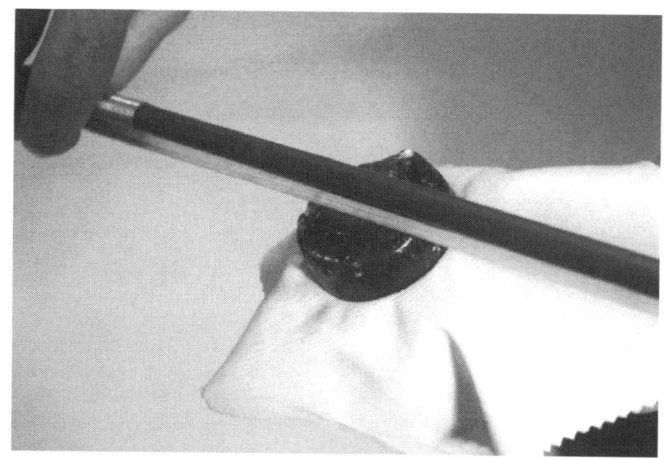

- Draw the bow back and forth several times across the rosin.

- Repeat whenever the hair gets slippery and unable to create good tone.

If the rosin is new, rough up the surface with some sandpaper (or a key or knife).

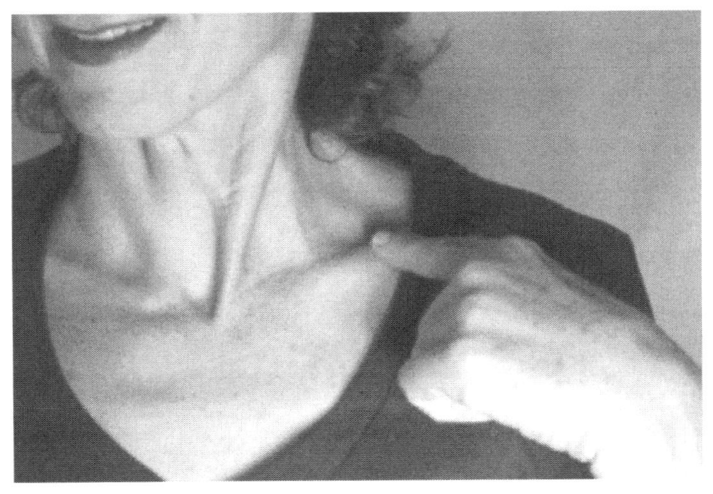

To hold the fiddle, rest the end of the fiddle here, on your left collarbone.

For a snug, secure hold, push the edge up against your neck.

To keep the fiddle from slipping down your chest, center the end on the "shelf" formed by your collarbone and shoulder ridge. The structure of this shoulder-collarbone "shelf" automatically rolls the fiddle somewhat inward.

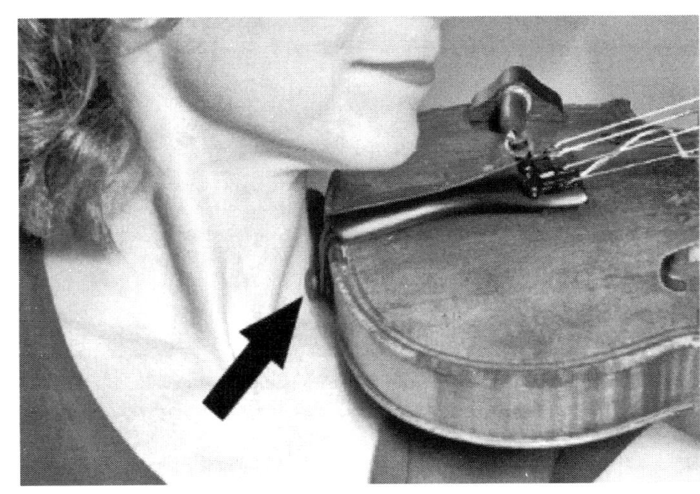

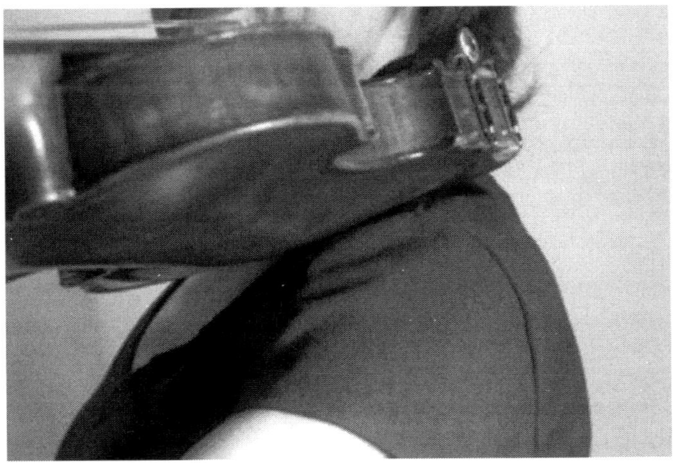

For free, balanced arm motion, keep your shoulders low and relaxed. Breathe expansively.

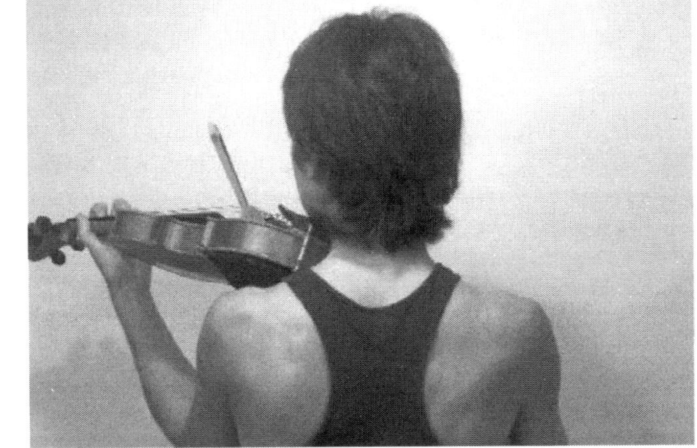

TO MAKE a GOOD SOUND

- Sweet spot (about 1/2 way between bridge and fingerboard)
- Keep the bow perpendicular to the string
- Optimum ratio of bow speed to pressure

Here's an easy "quick start" bow hold:

- Place your thumb under the frog.
- Lay the middle segments of the first three fingers on the stick.

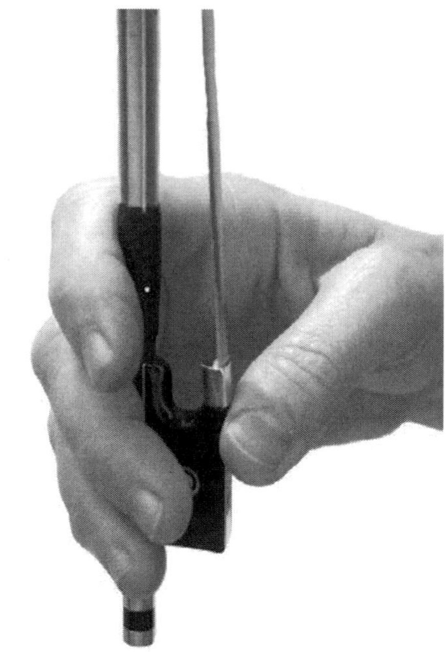

Just for now, so you can easily hold the fiddle and see what you're doing:

- Place the end of the fiddle against your chest.
- Hold it so the strings are level from nut to bridge.

Draw the bow back and forth.

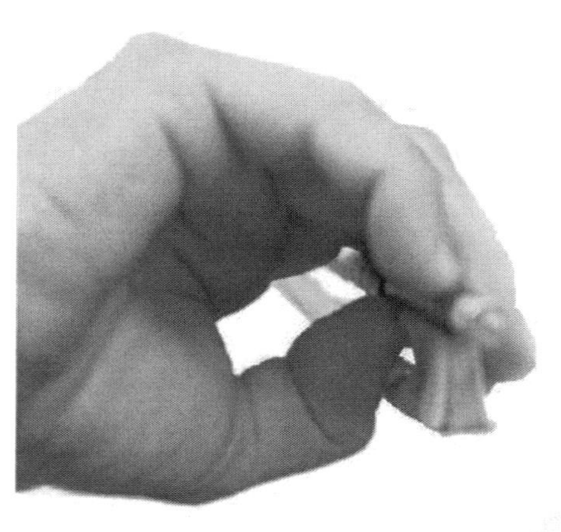

Here's the standard bow hold if you prefer.

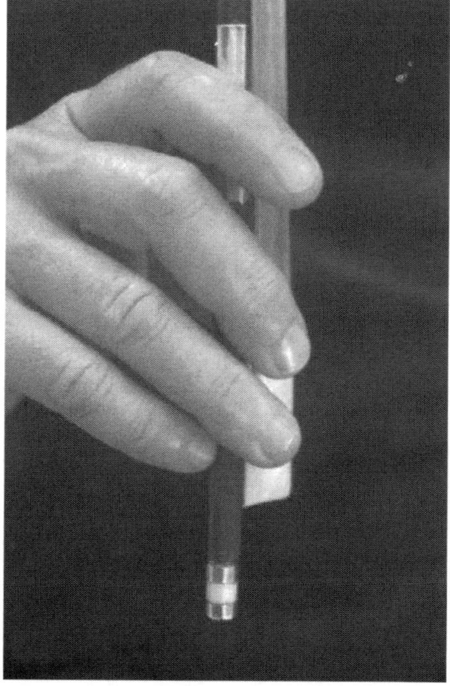

The OPEN STRINGS

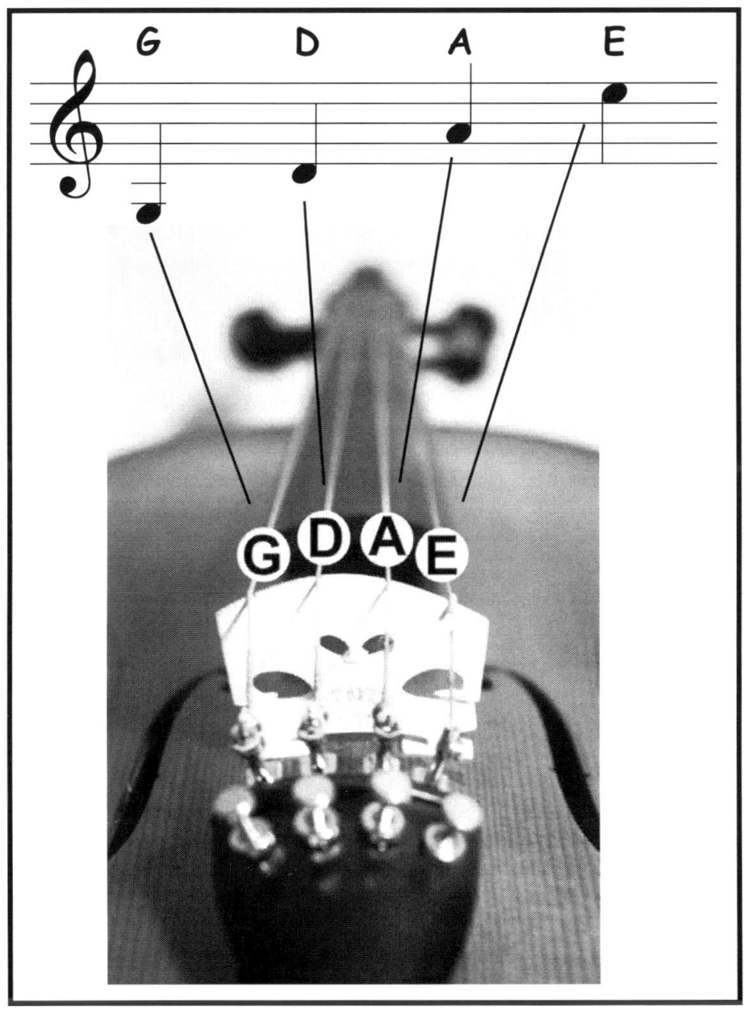

Hold the fiddle with your left hand anywhere on the neck, keeping your fingers off the strings. Set the bow on the strings, letting your elbow settle comfortably just below the level of your wrist. Make a right angle with your elbow.

Keeping that frame, silently raise and lower your arm to pivot the bow and position it over each string in turn (keep your shoulders down):

E String Position

A String Position

D String Position

G String Position

SAWSTROKE on the OPEN STRINGS

Play four quarter notes on each open string (no fingers down), going from the G (lowest) to the E (highest). Note that "low" and "high" refer to the pitch (sound) rather than physical position.

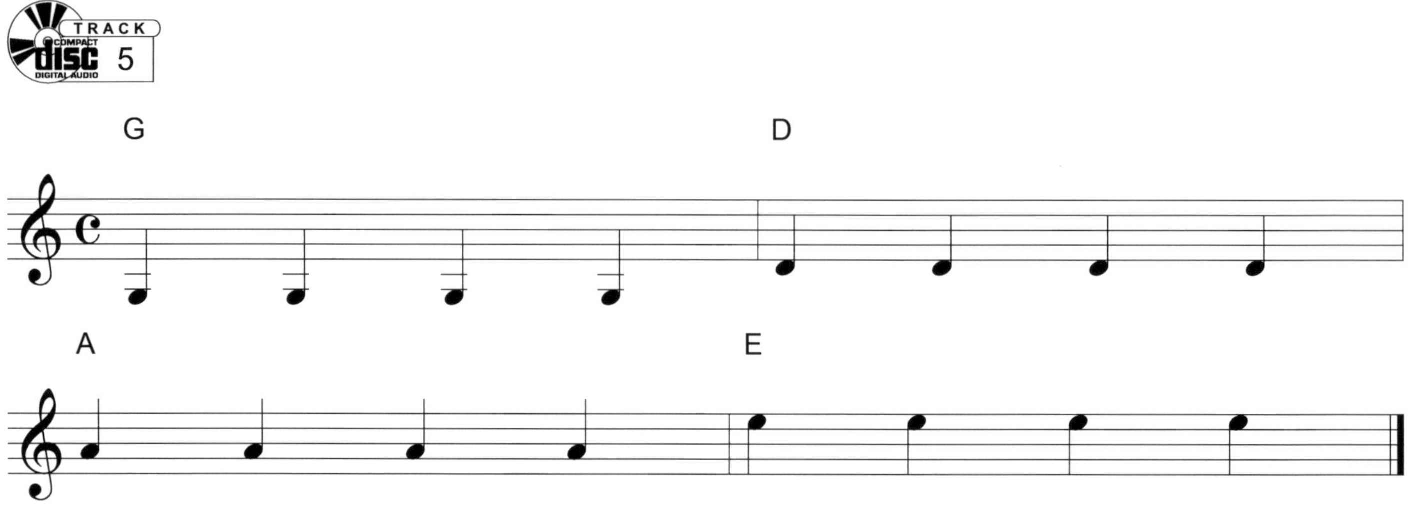

AFTER PLAYING

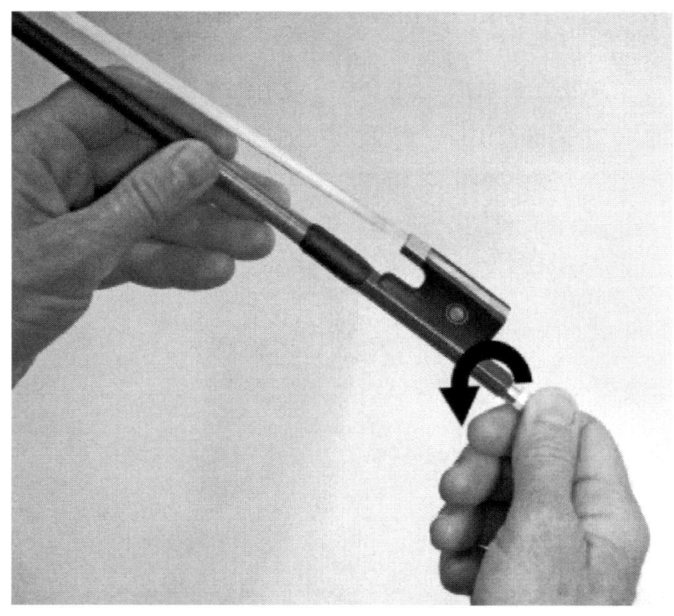

Loosen the bow hair:

Turn the screw counterclockwise until the hair just touches the stick at the middle.

This keeps the hair from breaking if the temperature or humidity changes.

NOTE NAMES

The notes are named using the first seven letters of the alphabet. They are written on a *staff* (see the next page).

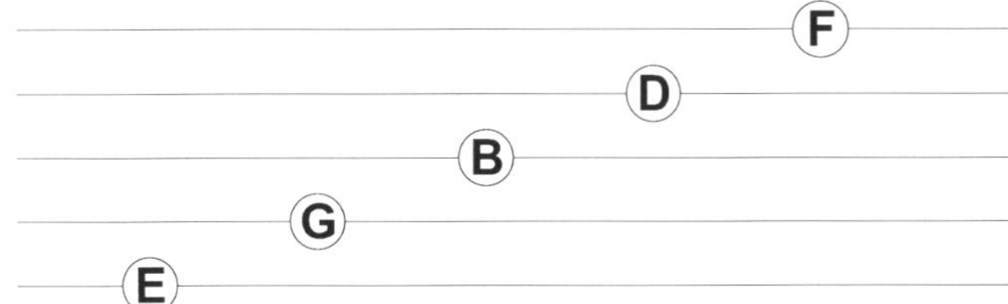

Play the notes on the lines with the 1st and 3rd (see page 14) fingers.

"Every Good Boy Does Fine"

Play the notes on the spaces with the 2nd and 4th fingers, or open strings.

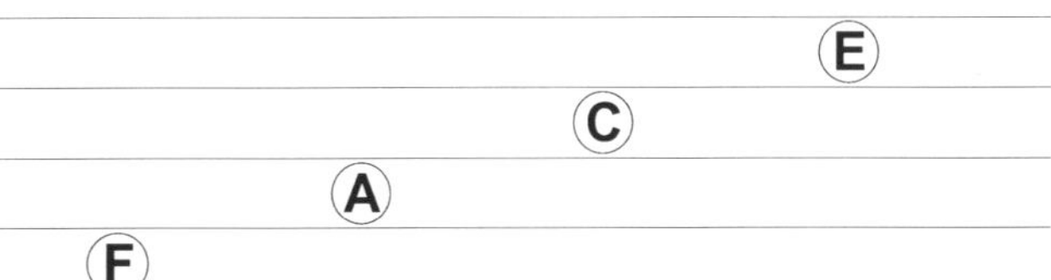

NOTE DURATIONS

NOTES		RESTS
𝅝	A whole note or rest = 4 counts, or *beats*	
𝅗𝅥	A half note or rest = 2 beats	
♩	A quarter note or rest = 1 beat	𝄽
♪	An eighth note or rest = 1/2 beat	𝄾
♫	Two eighth notes or rests = 1 beat	𝄾 𝄾

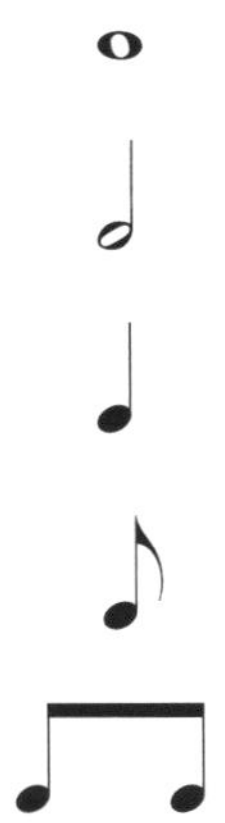

Count: one two three four

Count: one and two and three and four and

READING MUSIC

A *note* (𝅗𝅥) represents a musical sound.

Notes are written on a *staff*.

A note's *pitch* (highness or lowness) is indicated by its vertical placement on the staff's *lines* and *spaces*.

This note has a higher pitch than this one.

The G string has a lower pitch than the E. On any given string, notes closer to the bridge are higher (in pitch) than notes closer to the nut. Pitch is designated by the first seven letters of the alphabet, ascending respectively from A through G.

In fiddle music, you'll find a *treble clef* (𝄞) at the beginning of the staff. Its curlicue wraps around the second line from the bottom, designating that line as G.

Ledger lines are placed above or below the staff to extend its range as needed.

This "C" time signature stands for "common", or 4/4 time.
It also looks like this: 4/4

In 4/4 (common) time, these all equal four beats:

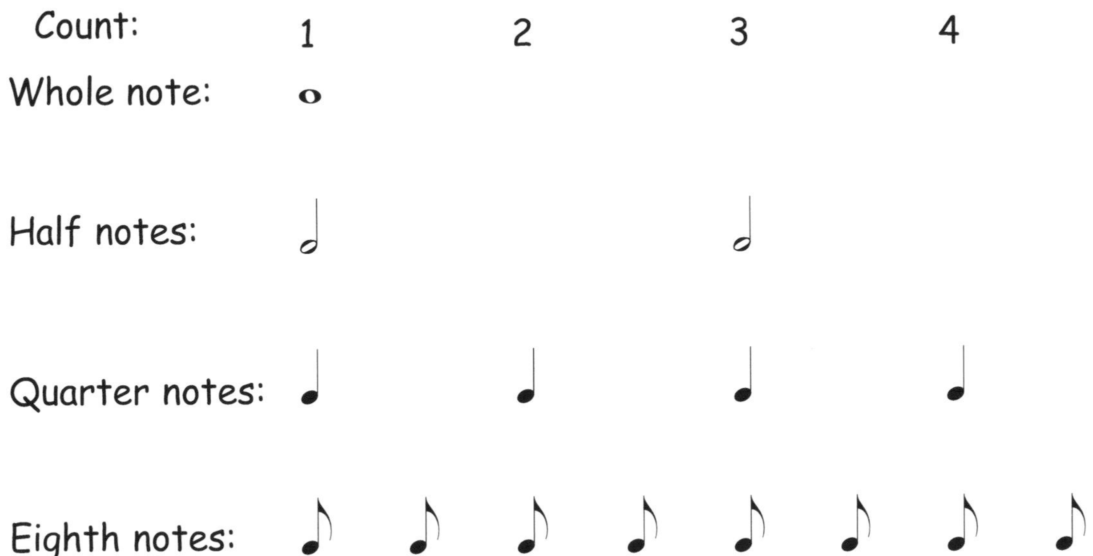

Sets of two or four eighth notes can be grouped by a *beam*:

Count: 1 and 2 and 3 and 4 and

A *measure* or bar is a group of beats. In most tunes, all the measures contain the same number of beats.

Each measure is enclosed by a pair of vertical *barlines*:

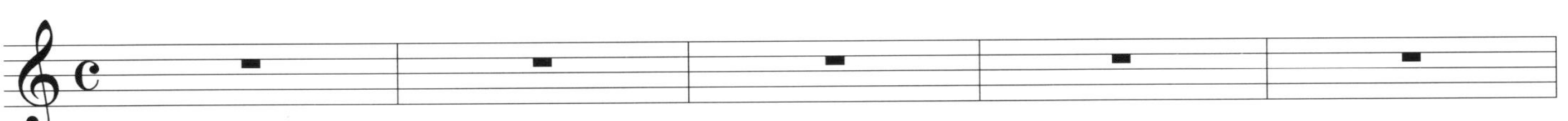

The number of beats per measure (in this case four) is indicated by the top number of the time signature.

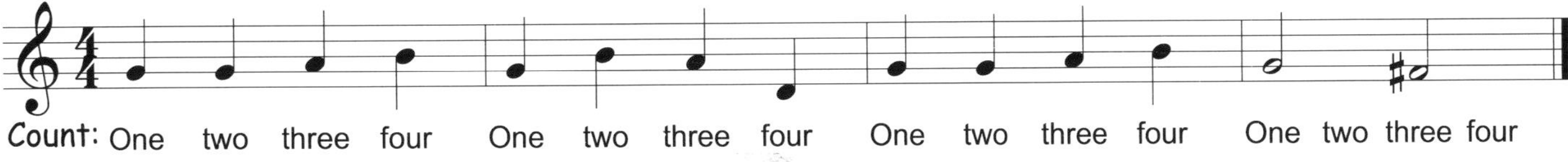

In 3/4 time, each measure contains three beats (the equivalent of three quarter notes).

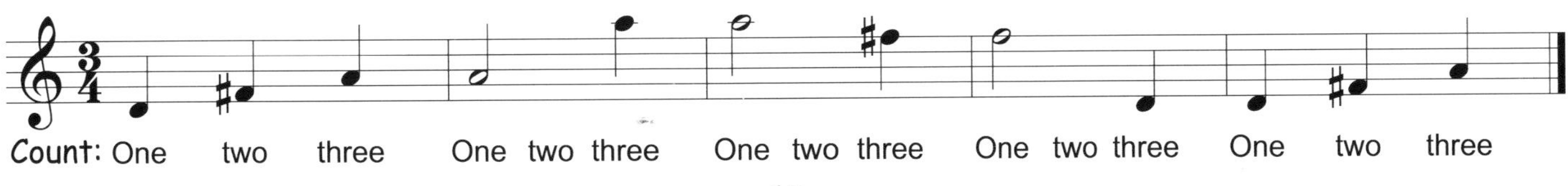

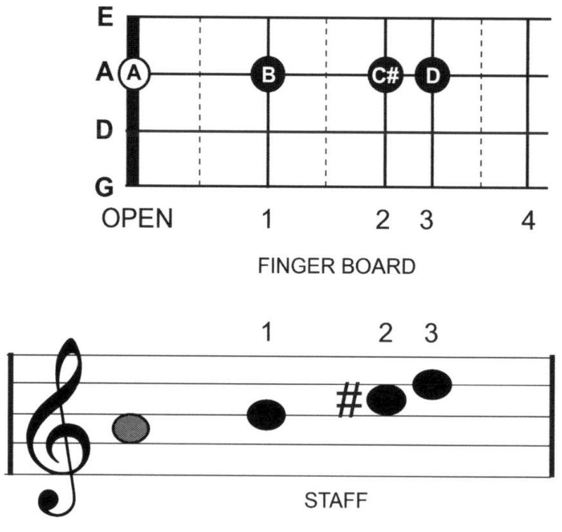

NOTES ON THE A STRING

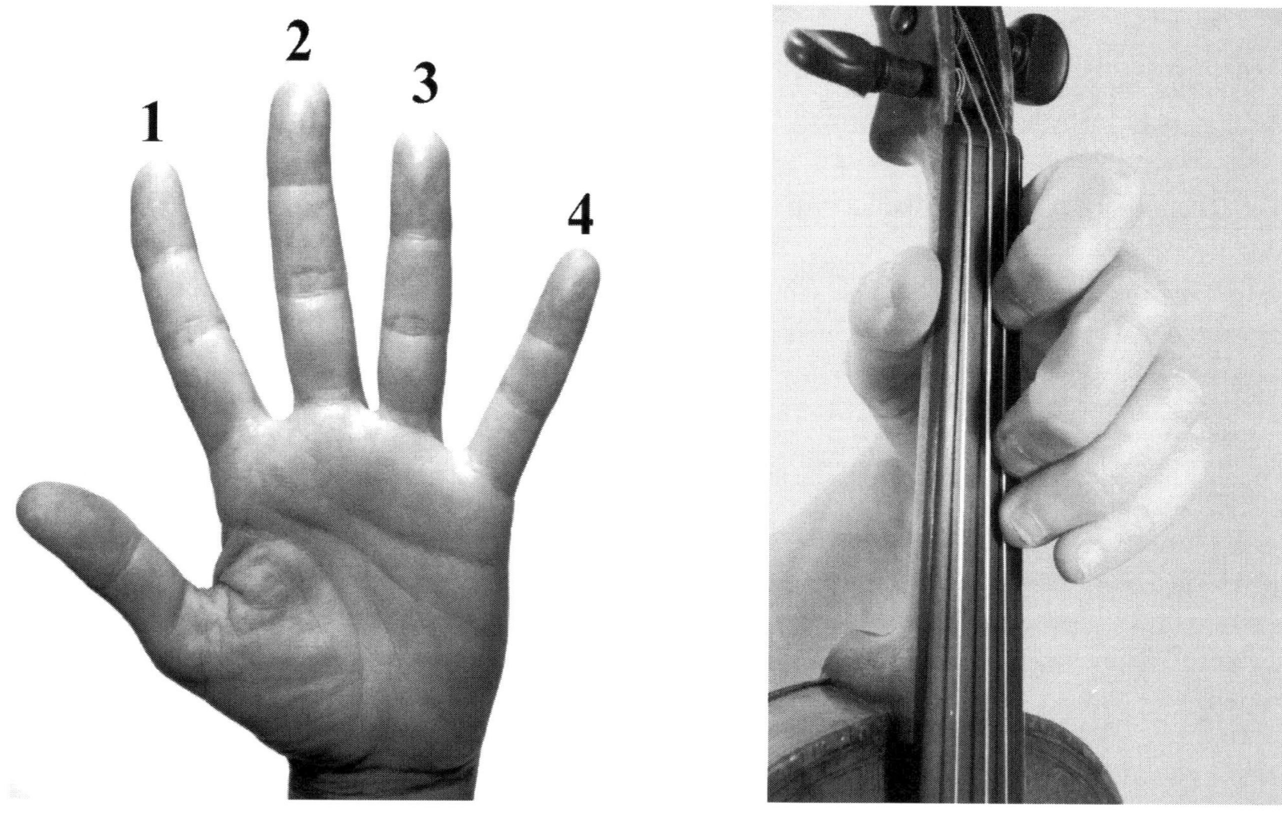

Finger Numbers

"Fretboard" overlays are available online.

ACCURATE INTONATION

(Precision of pitch)

- Balance the hand around the middle fingers.
- Lightly "anchor" the side of your forefinger to the side of the neck.
- Drop the fingertips directly onto the string.
- Match each note to a tuner or aural reference until your fingers automatically "find" the correct pitches.

LEFT HAND POSITION

Swing your left elbow left or right to position your fingertips over the strings like this.

Keep an open circle under the neck.

You can think of it as holding the fiddle in the fork of a tree, without letting it slip down into the trough.

Hold it gently as though there was an egg resting on your palm.

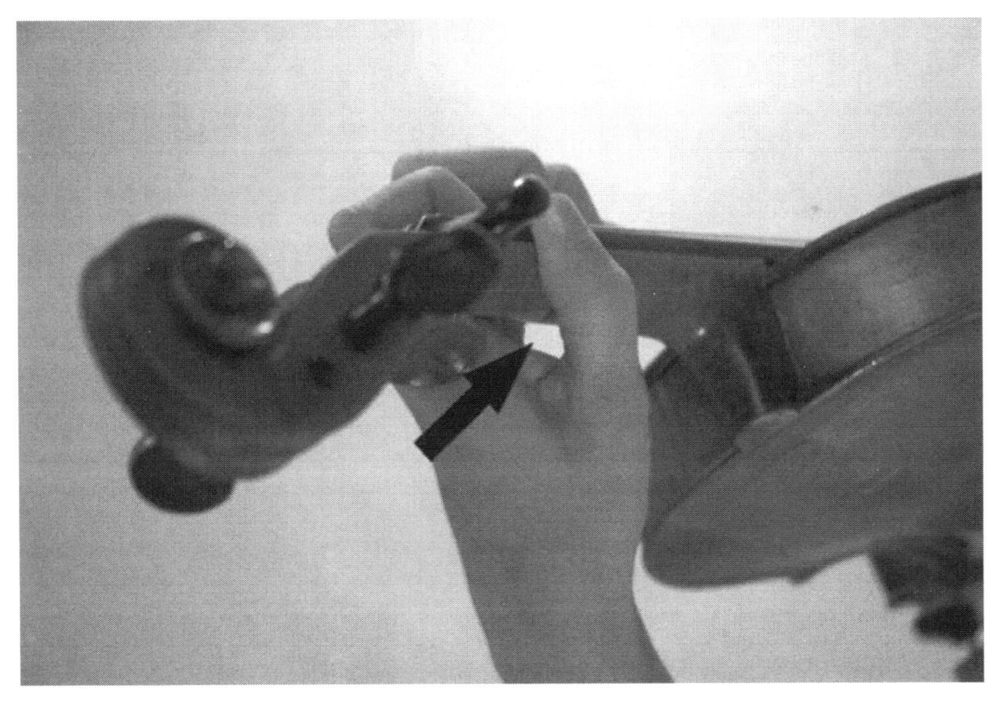

Keep your wrist straight.

HOT CROSS BUNS

To begin, you can hold the fiddle like a guitar and pluck these three notes on the A string:

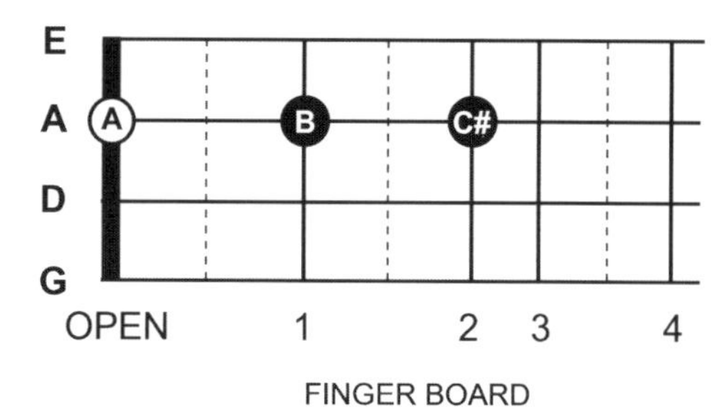

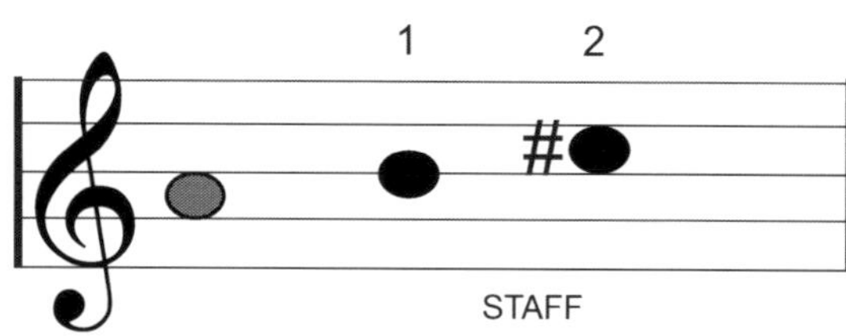

Avoid the bow path so oils from your fingers don't affect the performance of the rosin there.

- Brace your middle finger against the bottom edge of the fingerboard.
- Pluck with your thumb.

Now you can bow it. ⊓ = Downbow (pull the bow to the right).

SHUFFLE BOWING

Play this on your open D string. Alternate your bow direction at the beginning of each group of three.

Let your bow arm "dance."

See if you can tap your foot to keep time (two or four taps per measure).

BOIL the CABBAGE DOWN

The standard fiddle tune everybody knows!

Your notes will be on the D string now:

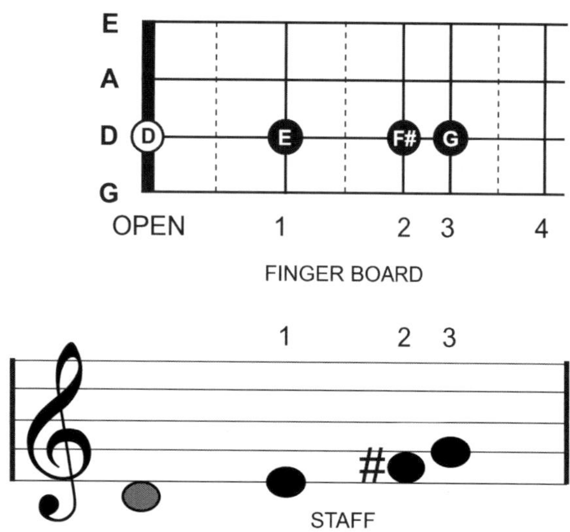

Notice lines 1 and 3 are alike.

The pattern changes on the last line – you play only one set of three for each pitch, and at the end you add a final quarter note.

The letters above the staff are *chords* for a backup player.

TRACK COMPACT disc DIGITAL AUDIO 8

D G

D A

D G

D A D

BOIL the CABBAGE DOWN with DRONES

When you see two notes stacked one on top of the other, play them together. In this case you'll play both middle strings throughout the entire tune.

Drone the open A as you note with your fingers on the D string. Pivot your left elbow to the right, to roll your fingers to the left side of the D string so you clear that A.

You can leave your second finger down the whole time except for bar 4 and at the end.

BOIL the CABBAGE DOWN on the A STRING

Now let's transpose it from the key of D to the key of A.

For a real fiddle "drive" you can push and pull the bow extra fast on beats 2 and 4 of each bar to accent them.

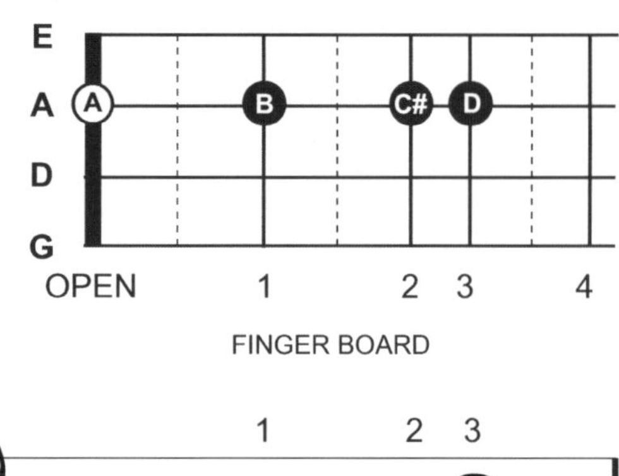

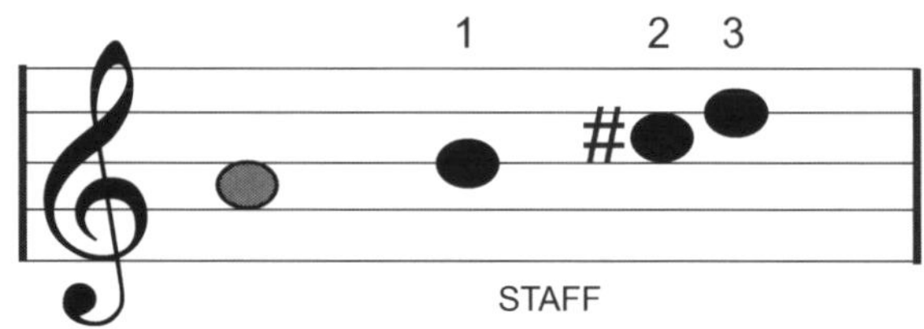

TRACK 10

A D

A E

A D

A E A

BOIL the CABBAGE DOWN on the TOP TWO STRINGS

Now drone the open E throughout.

MARY HAD a LITTLE LAMB

The "0" in bar 4 refers now to the open E string. "Scoop" your right elbow to the left to cross to it.

Sustain the half notes on "lamb" for two counts in bars 2, 3 and 4. The whole note in the last bar gets four counts.

A E A A E A

Ma - ry had a lit - tle lamb,
lit - tle lamb, lit - tle lamb,
Ma - ry had a lit - tle lamb; its
fleece was white as snow.

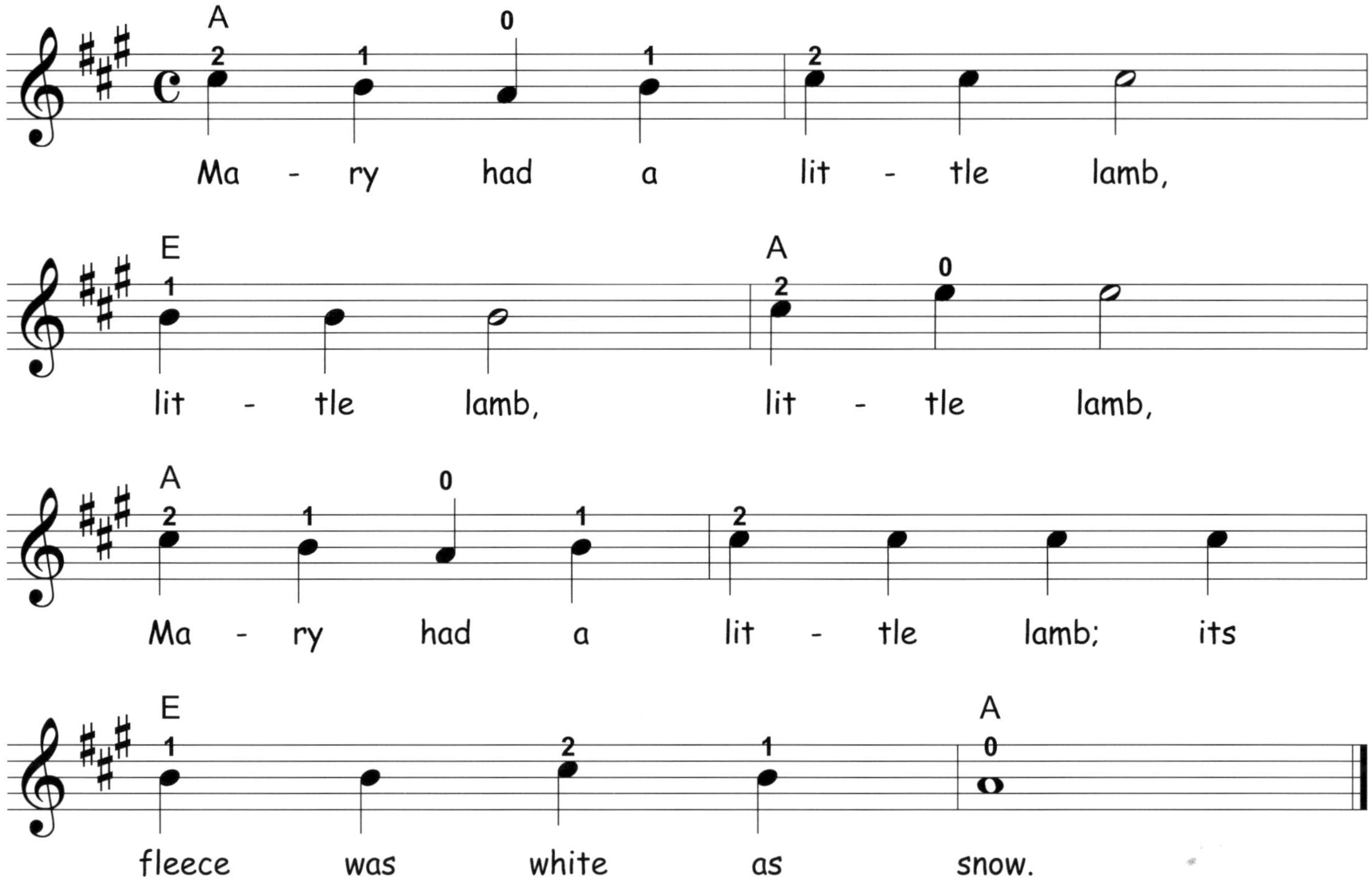

ANGELINE the BAKER

This tune is played mostly on the D string. It's in the key of G. Keep your bow on the string for the quarter rest in bar 2. Lift it at the ' symbol for the half rest in bar 4.

Hold the *dotted* quarter notes (♩.) for one and a half counts.

CRIPPLE CREEK

This tune has two new notes on the E string:

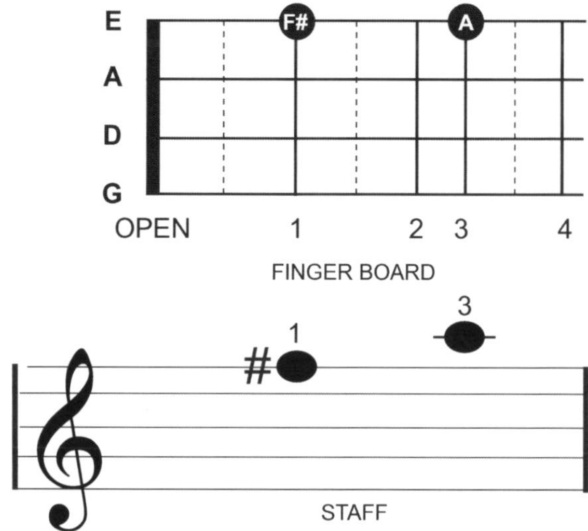

There are two sections. Section A repeats back to the beginning, as indicated by the repeat sign (:II) at the end of it. Section B is enclosed between a pair of repeat signs; when you get to the last one go back to the first.

Notice the second halves of both sections are the same. Raise your right elbow to dip over to the D string in the last bar of each.

TRACK 14

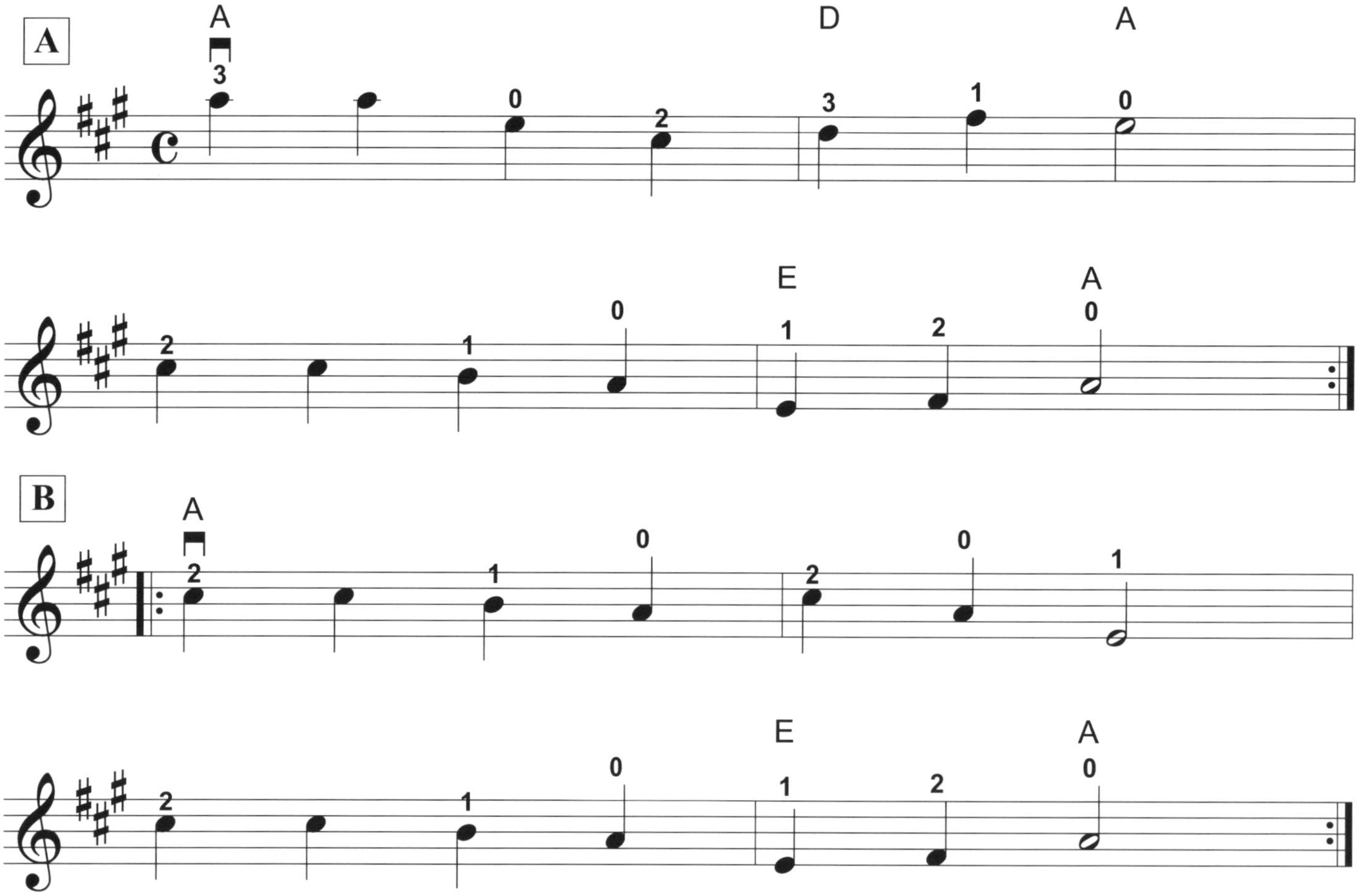

A

A D A

E A

B

A

E A

CRIPPLE CREEK
with SHUFFLE BOWING and DRONES

After the first line, let's add drones to the rest of the tune.

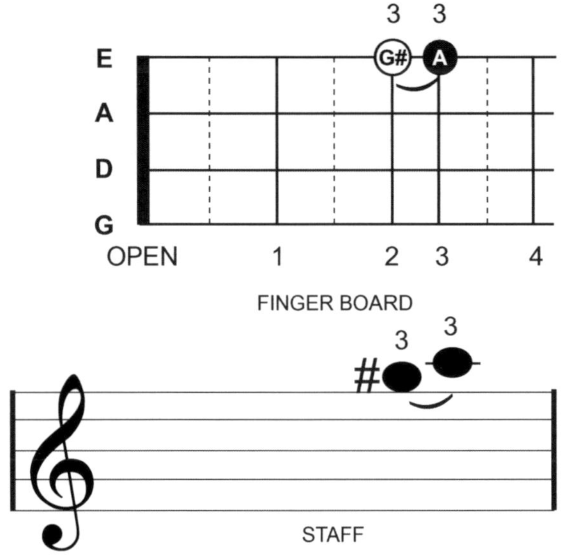

3rd Finger Slide on the E String

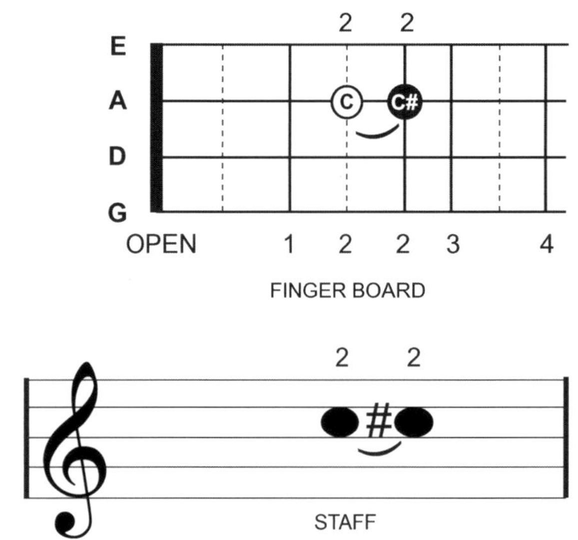

2nd Finger Slide on the A String

CRIPPLE CREEK with SLIDES

You can slide (/) into the first note of each phrase. Start before the beat with your finger about a half inch below (toward the peg box) the target note. Slide into the target note, timing it to land on the beat. You can add shuffle bowing and drones too.

TRACK 16

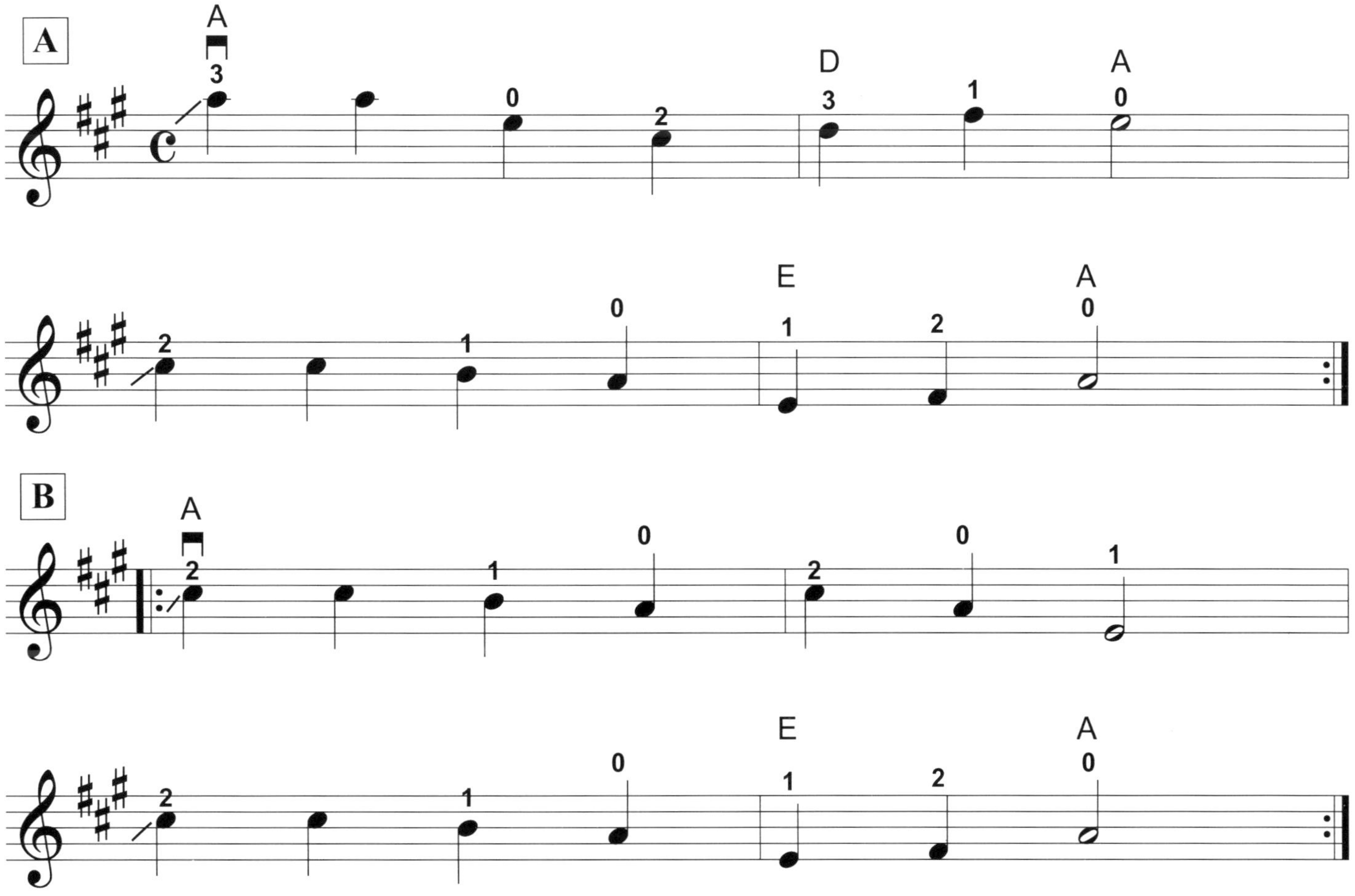

A

A D A

E A

B

A

E A

INTRO to CRIPPLE CREEK

Now you can add this "4 taters" intro.

TRACK 17

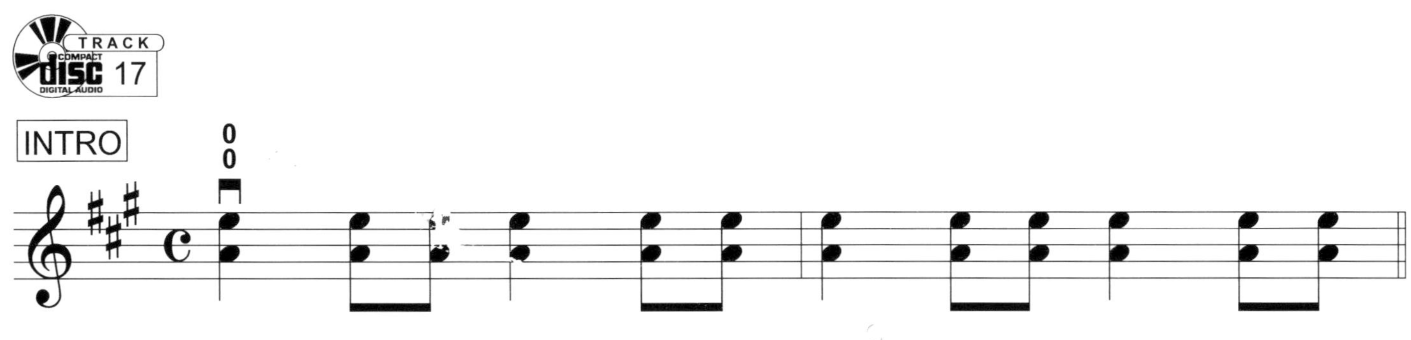

TRACK 18 Cripple Creek with Everything (Intro and Melody)

McNAB'S HORNPIPE - DIPPING the BOW

Here the A and B sections don't repeat. The song starts with two *pickup notes*, leading into it before the downbeat.

Dipping the bow is used as an effect here in bars 1, 3 and 5 (counting from the first full bar) of Section A and also in Section B. Raise your right elbow to dip over to the A string for these.

Your 2nd finger will remain in the regular position (touching the 3rd) on the A string but will be in the *low* position (touching the 1st) for the G natural on the E.

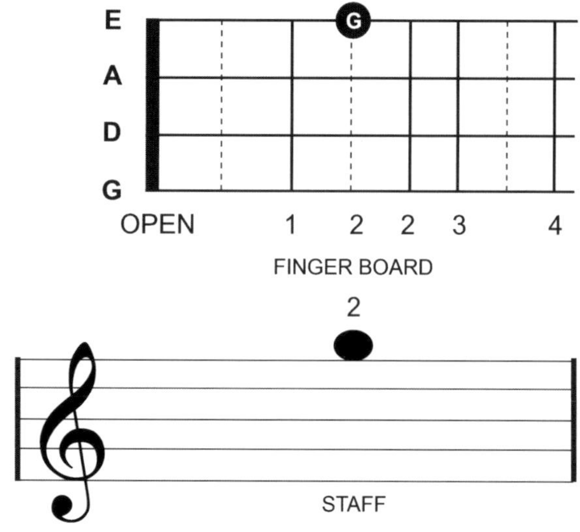

Leave your 1st and 2nd fingers down as much as possible.

McNAB'S HORNPIPE - ROCKING the BOW

Rock the bow back and forth between the E and A strings by making circles with your right hand, where you dipped the bow before. Keep your wrist loose to make it smooth.

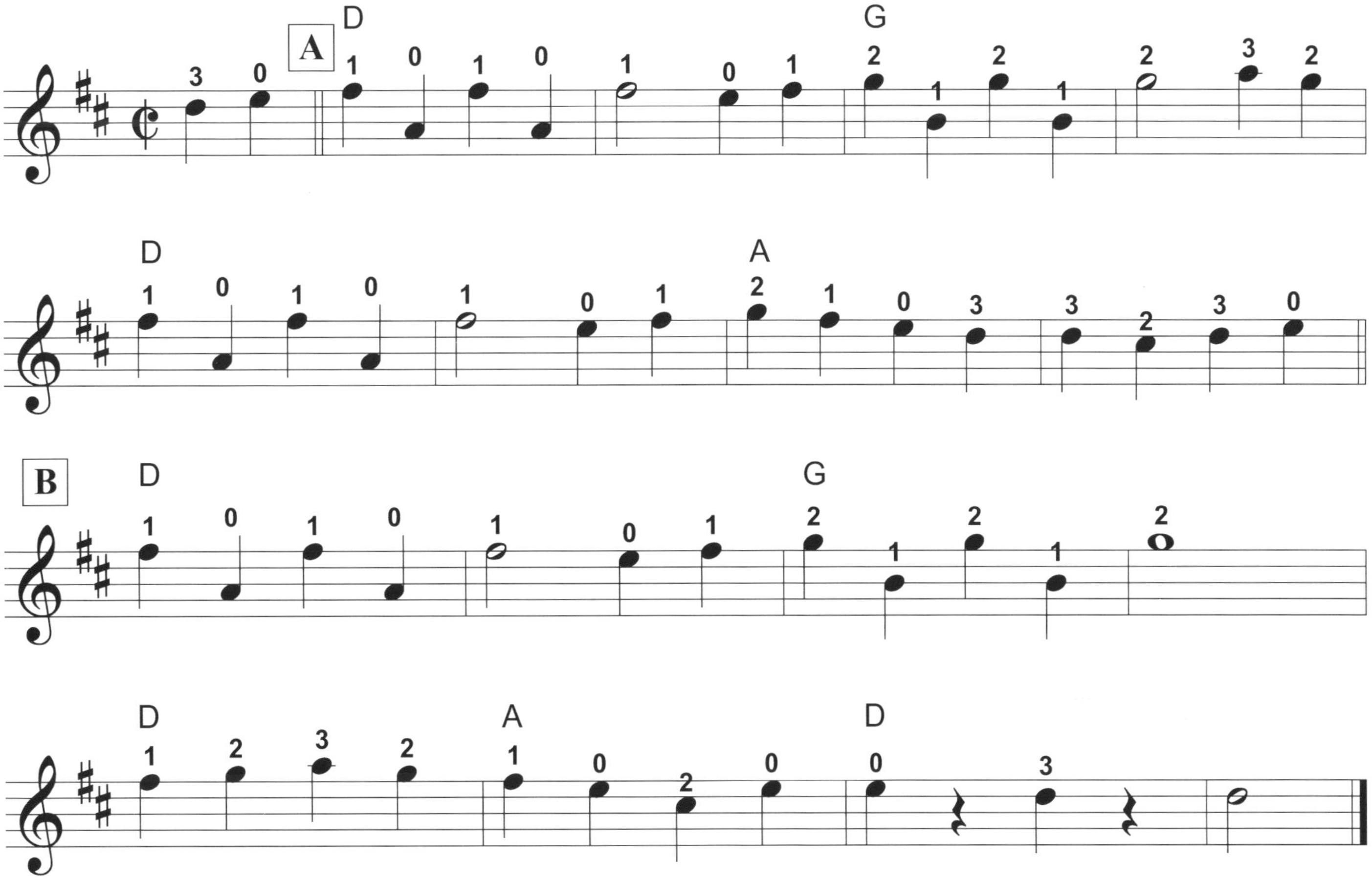

LIZA JANE

Now we'll rock the bow on 8th notes, making smaller circles with the right hand.

Leave your 3rd finger down as much as you can, as indicated by the 3------s

Notice bars 1 and 3 are alike.

Bars 2 and 4 are *syncopated;* the second note spans beat two, rather than landing directly on it.

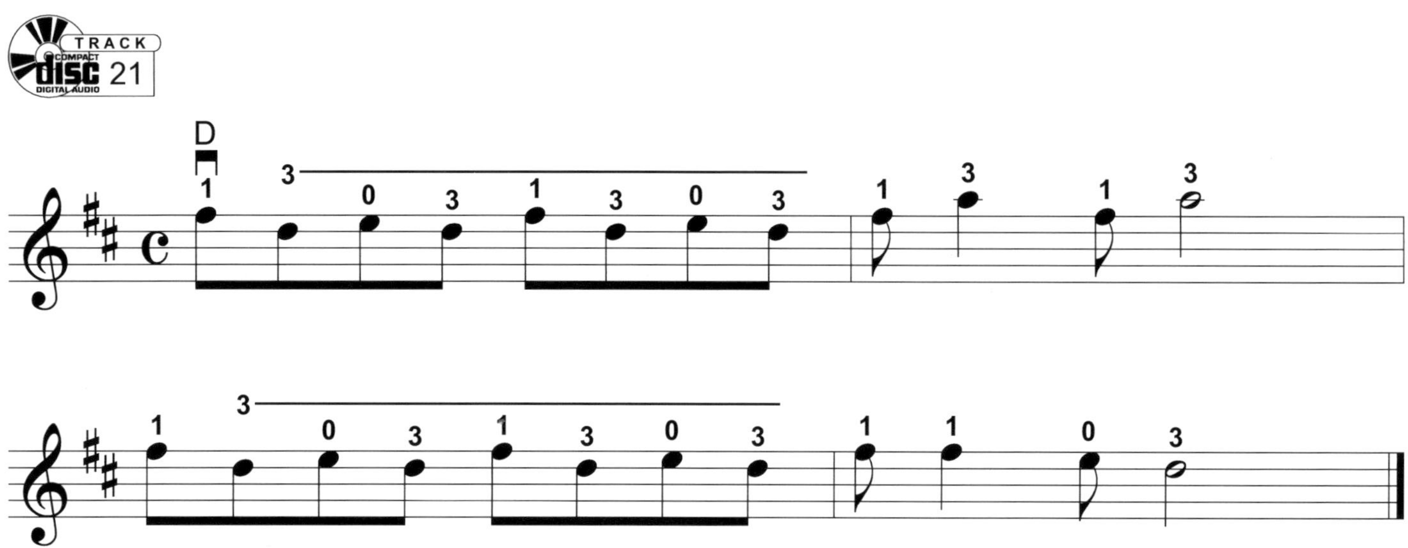

LIZA JANE FANCY VERSION

Now let's dress it up with shuffle bowing and drones. You can add 1st finger slides if you like.

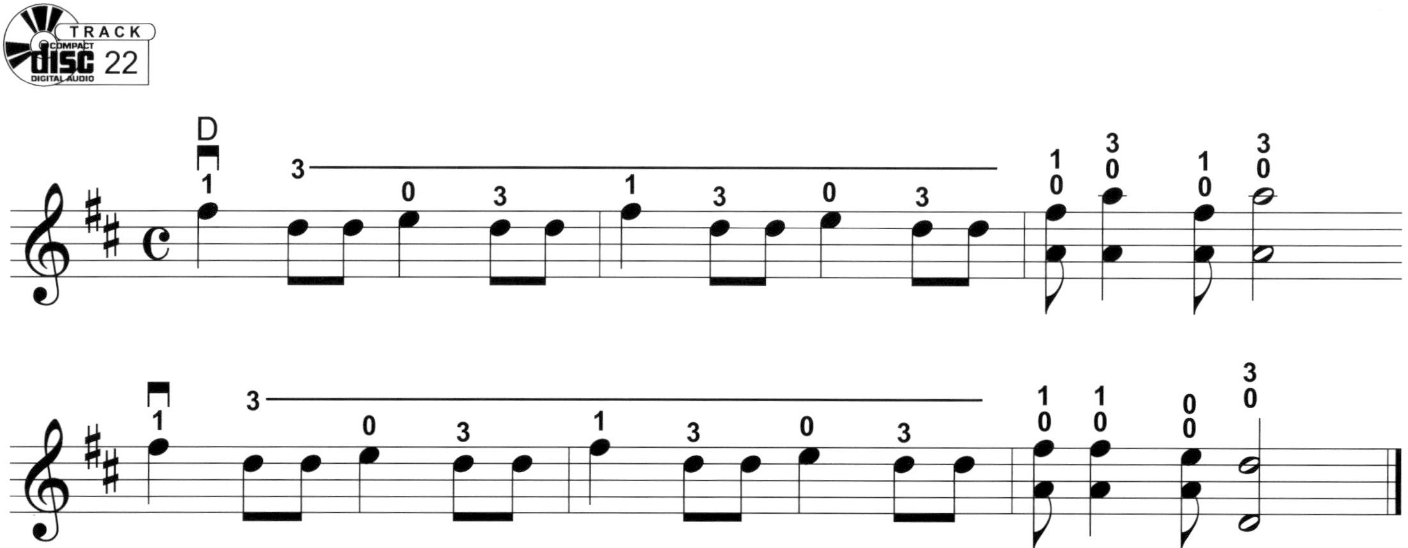

OLD JOE CLARK

This is a *modal* tune, as opposed to a *major* key like all the others so far. It's in A but uses G natural rather than G♯, putting it in A *Mixolydian.*

TRACK 23

OLD JOE CLARK
with HAMMER-ONS and PULL-OFFS

We'll slur (⌒ : play together in the same bow stroke) the two notes of these ornaments. Note that you are playing shuffle bowing (long-short-short) throughout, whether it's a single quarter or two eighth notes on the long bow.

At the beginning of the first three lines of each section, connect the open string in one bow to the 1st finger hammer-on. You can leave that 1st finger down the second time, as you go to the 2nd finger. Then pull-off that 2nd finger, slurring it into the following note. We have a new drone—the open G string—in Section B, measure 4. Raise your right elbow to sound both the G and D strings.

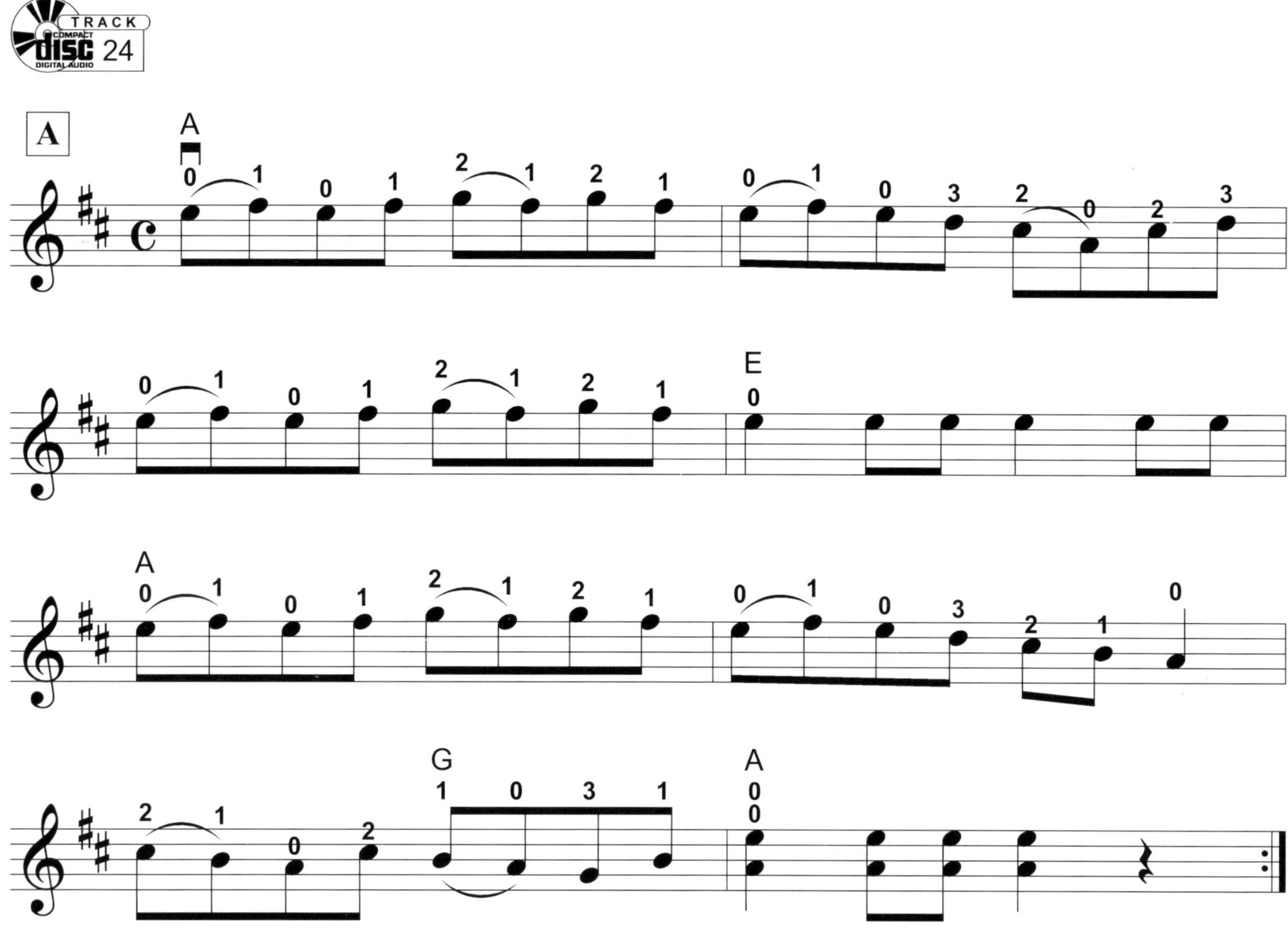

B
A
0 1 0 1 2 0 2 3 0 1 0 3 2 1 0
0 1 0 1 2 1 0 2
G
3
0
A
0 1 0 1 2 0 2 3 0 1 0 3 2 1 0
G
2 1 0 2 1 0 3 1
A
0
0

TRACK 25

OLD JOE CLARK
with SHUFFLE BOWING and DRONES

You can also use these drones with the previous version.

RED-HAIRED BOY

This tune is also in A Mixolydian. Notice both sections end roughly the same. Give it a *swing* feel, playing the first note of each pair of eighths a bit longer and the second one a bit shorter than usual.

The slurs this time are into the beat instead of on it, another *swing bowing* technique.

Each section has a 1st and 2nd ending. At the 1st ending, go back to the beginning of the section. Next time skip to the 2nd ending.

POP! GOES the WEASEL

This is a *jig*, in 6/8 time (count "1-2-3 4-5-6" or simply "1-2") for each measure. When you see the "+" symbols in the second to last bar, pluck the open E, then A with your left pinkie. This will start strengthening that finger.

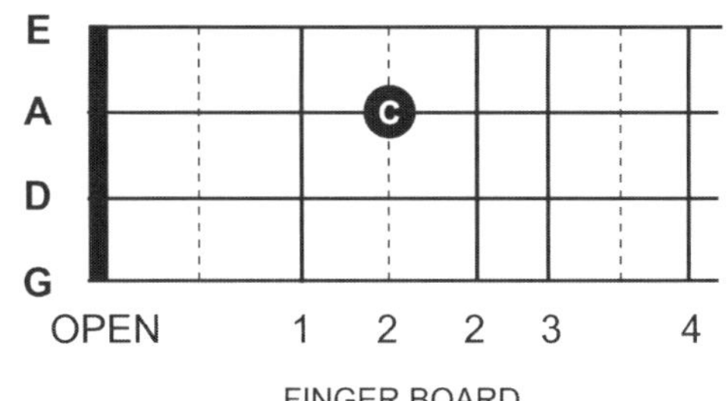

Play the 2nd finger on the A string in the low position, touching the first.

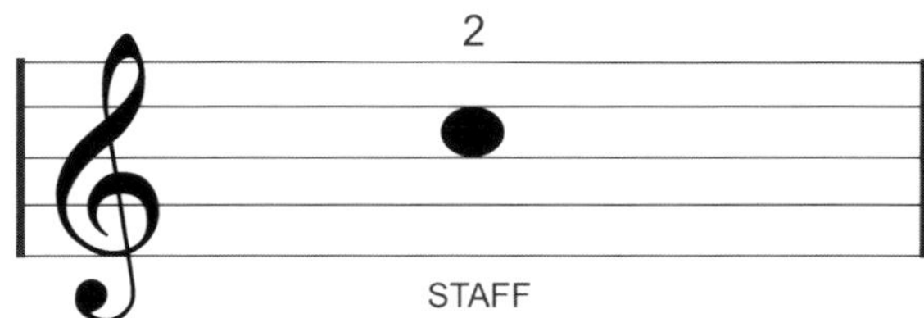

SOLDIER'S JOY

You will find pairs of slurred upbow (V - push the bow to the left) pickup notes leading into the next bar throughout the song. The slurs correct the bowing to keep your main beats on a strong downbow.

In Section A bar 6 and Section B bar 4, you have a slurred string crossing. Drop your elbow to do it smoothly. You can give the bow an extra fast pull on beats two and four for a strong backbeat feel. Keep your 2nd finger in the normal high position on the A string but low on the E. Rock the bow smoothly in Section B.

TRACK
COMPACT
disc
DIGITAL AUDIO
28

SOLDIER'S JOY with 1-and-3 BOWING

Slur three notes where indicated. Give each preceding downbow an extra fast pull to equalize the bow strokes and emphasize the downbeats.

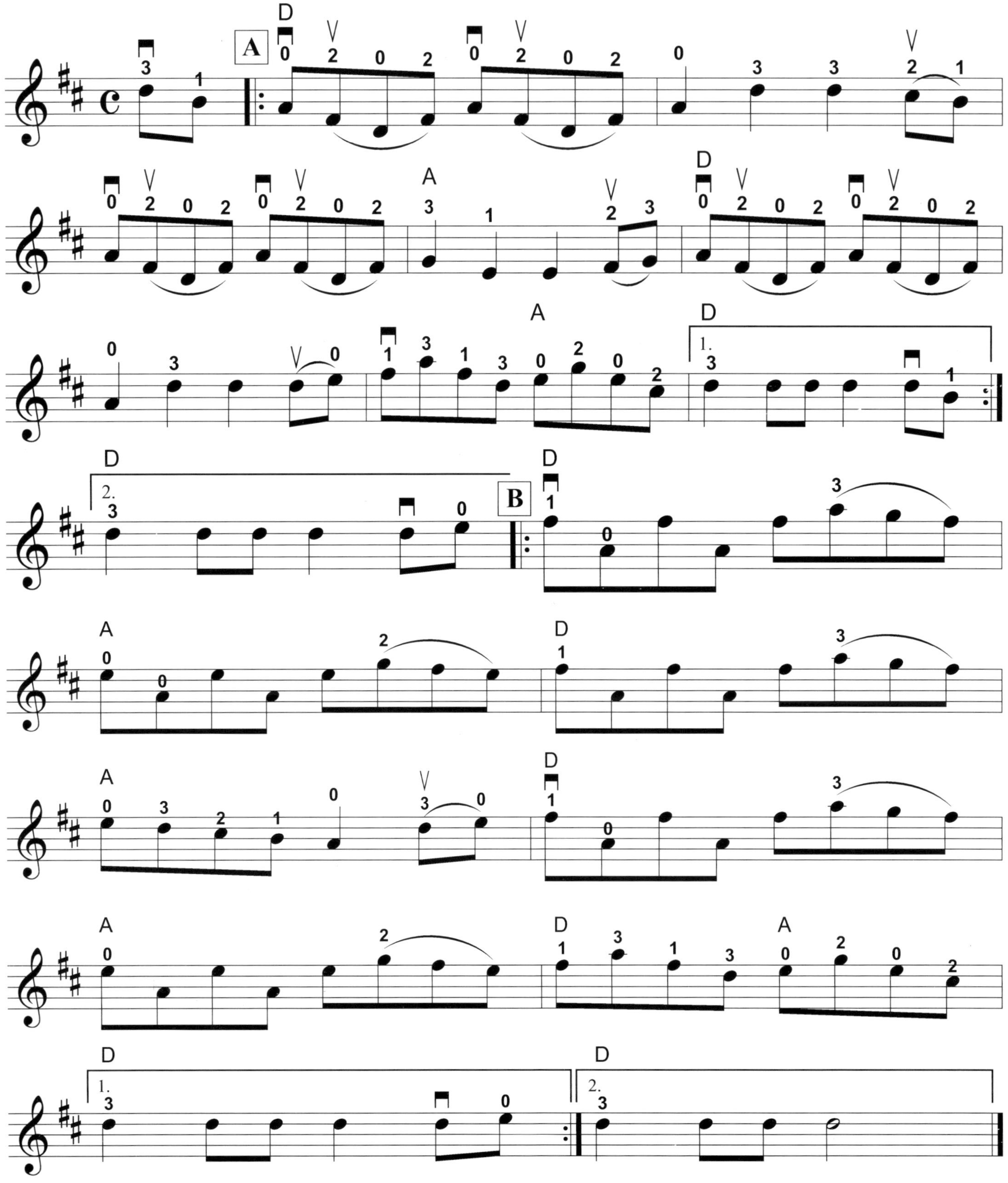

SOLDIER'S JOY with PROGRESSING LINES

While rocking the bow in Section B you can make a melodic line with the top notes as shown.

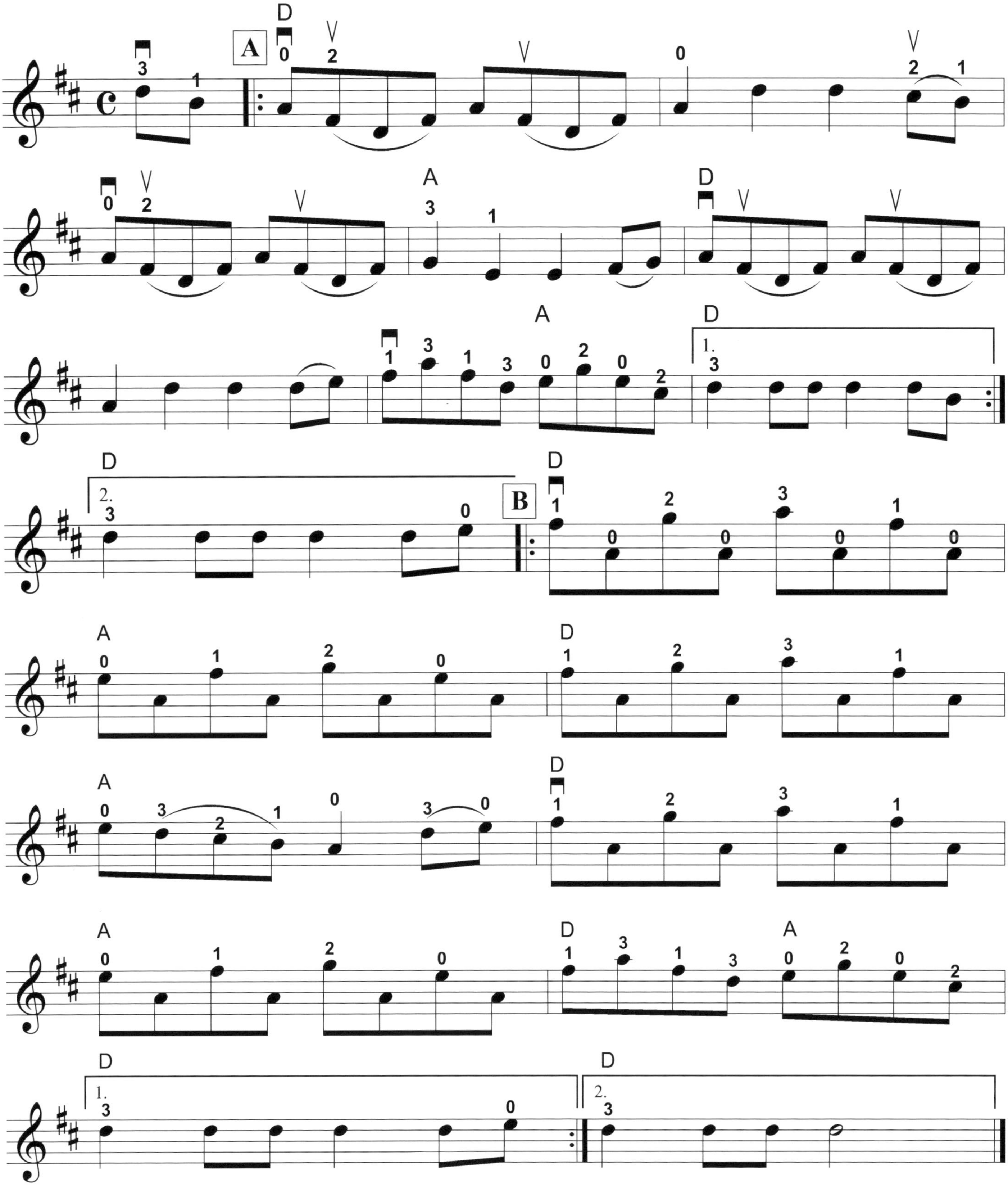

DEVIL'S DREAM

Play the 2nd finger in the high position (touching the 3rd) for the G♯ on the E string.

On the second note of bar 3 in both sections, mash your 1st finger down on both the A and E strings to cover B and F♯ together. Then toggle the 3rd finger down and up to alternate between D and B on the A string as you rock the bow, while leaving the 1st finger in place on both strings.

You have a *triplet rollup* pickup into the song.

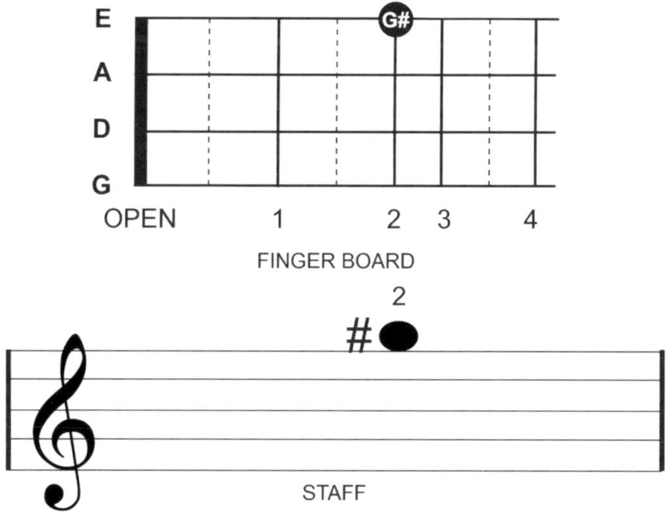

TRACK 31

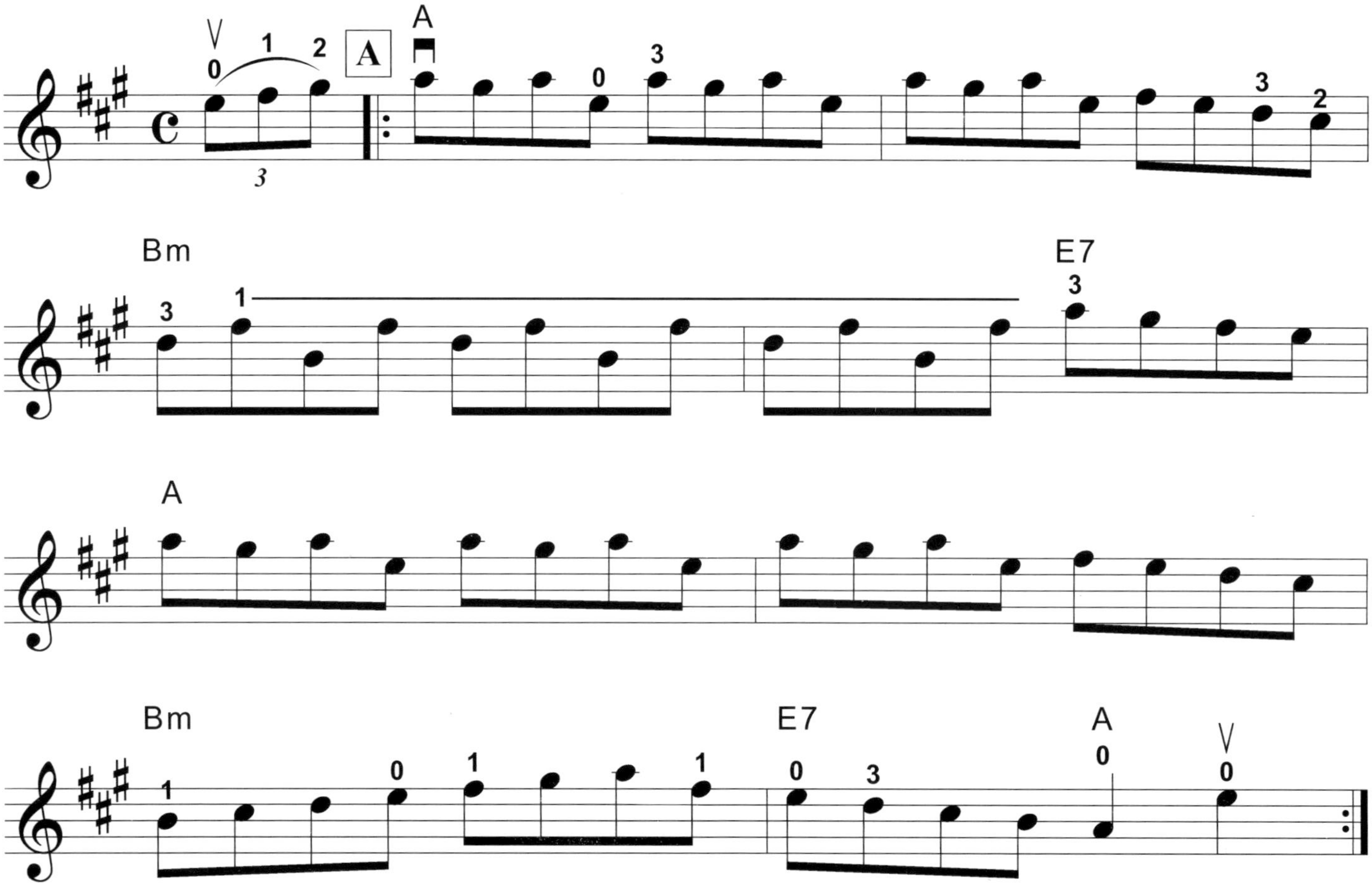

A

A

Bm

E7

A

Bm

E7

A

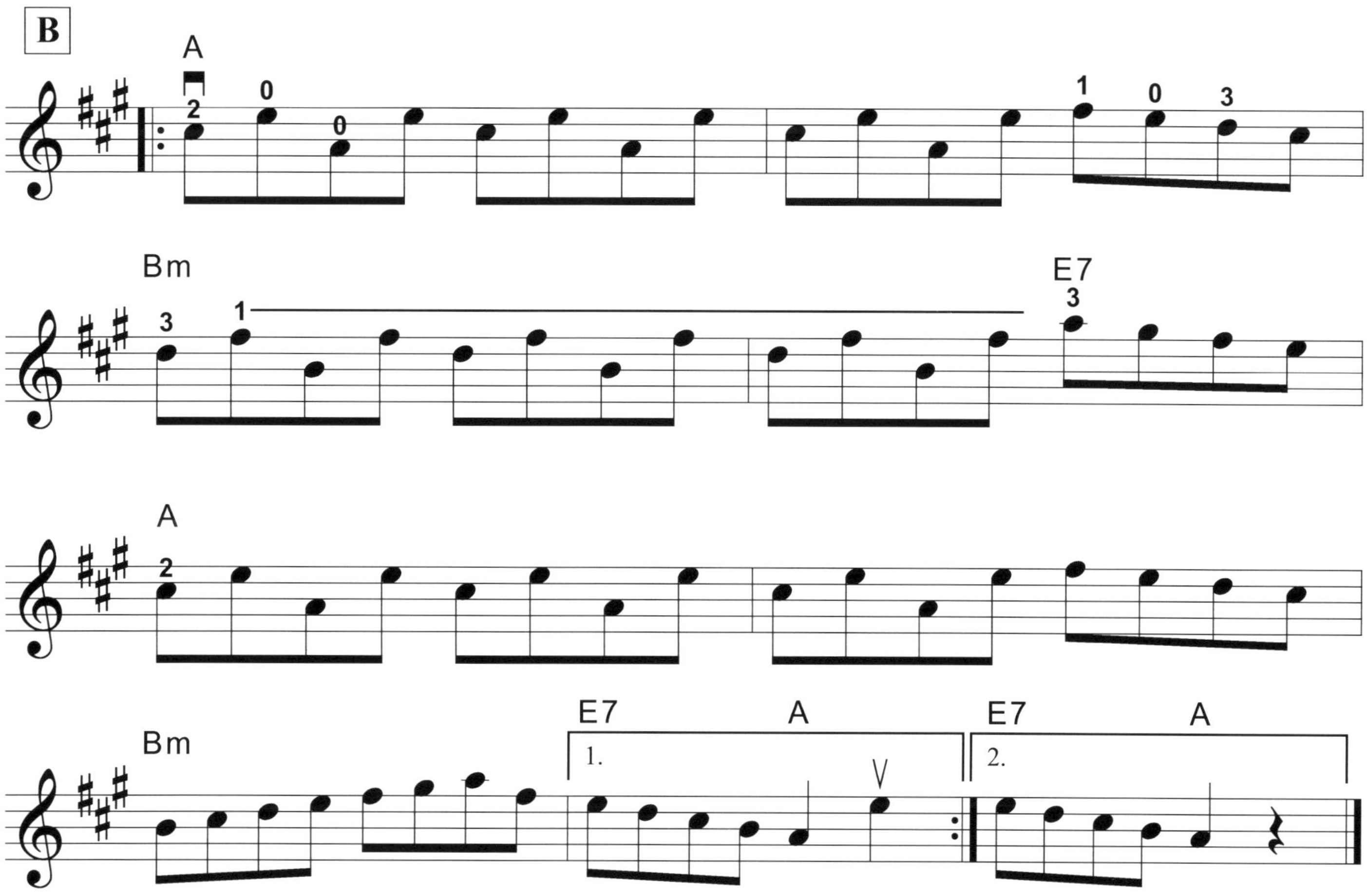

B

A Bm E7 A Bm E7 A E7 A

1. 2.

DEVIL'S DREAM TAG

You can complete the song with this tag.

ARKANSAS TRAVELER

Use your 4th finger on the A string to play E in Section B as noted. It will keep those passages all on the same string. It's the same pitch as open E.

Sections A and B end alike.

E
A
D
G
E
E
OPEN
1
2 3
4
FINGER BOARD

1
2 3
4
STAFF

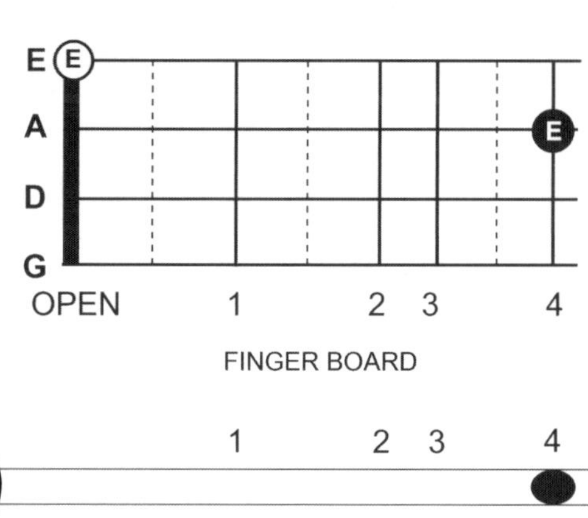

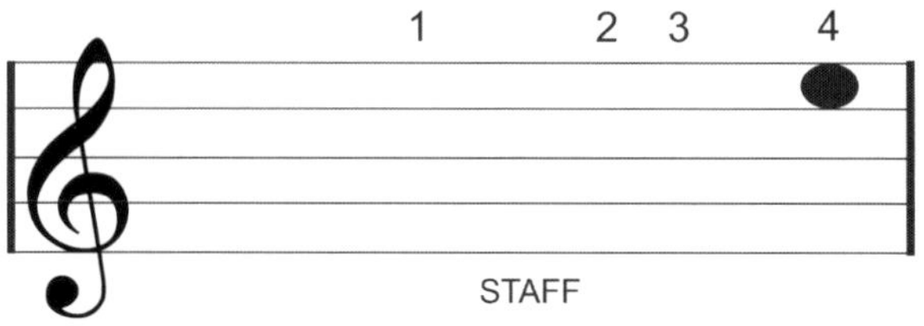

TRACK 33

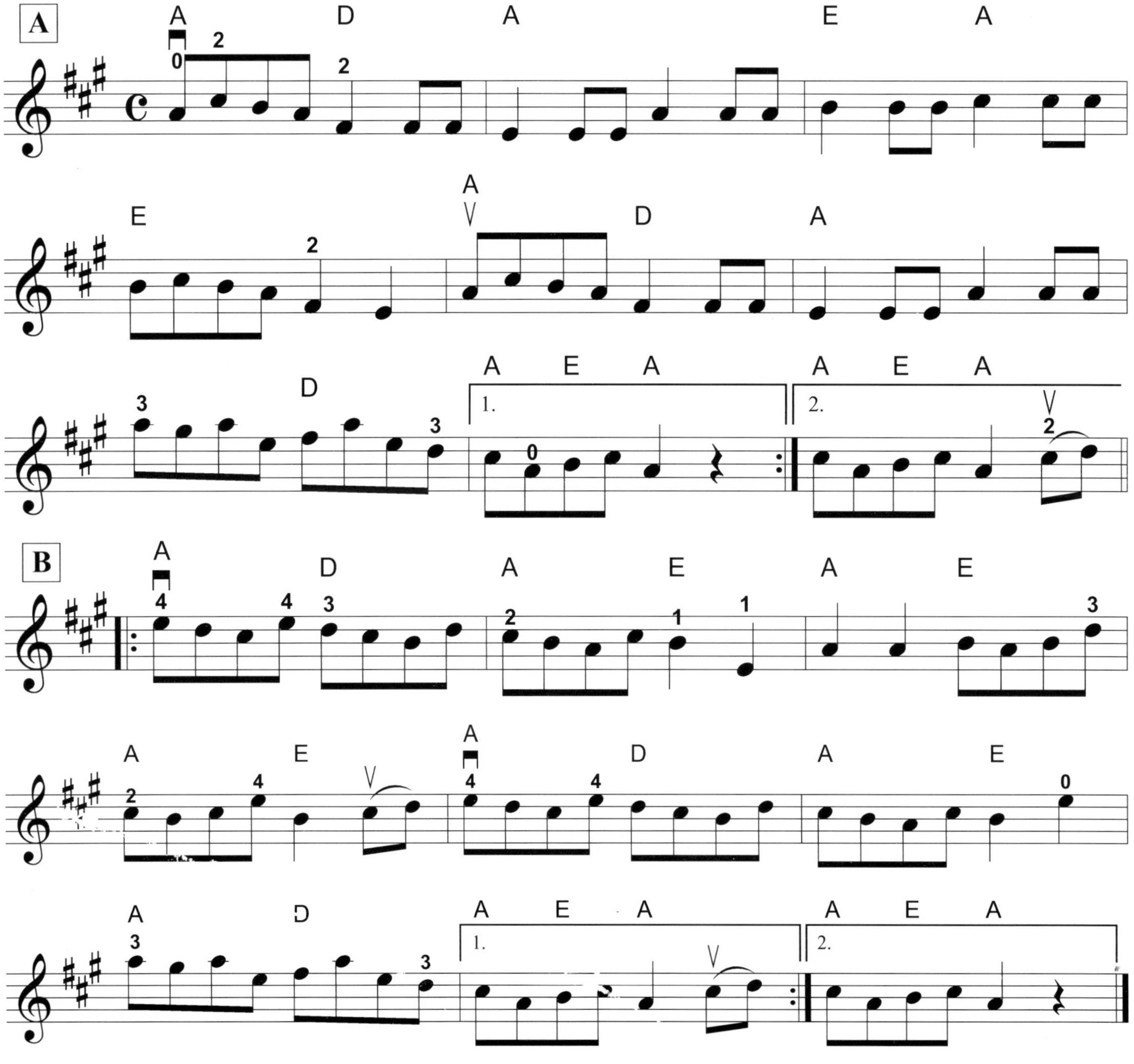

A
A D A E A
E A D A
D A E A A E A
1.
2.
B
A D A E A E
A E A D A E
A D A E A A E A
1.
2.

ST. ANNE'S REEL

Use your 4th finger on the E string to play B in Section B as noted. In Bar 3 of Section B, your 2nd finger will be high on the A string but low on the E. In the next bar it is high on the E string for the G♯, then low for the G natural (♮).

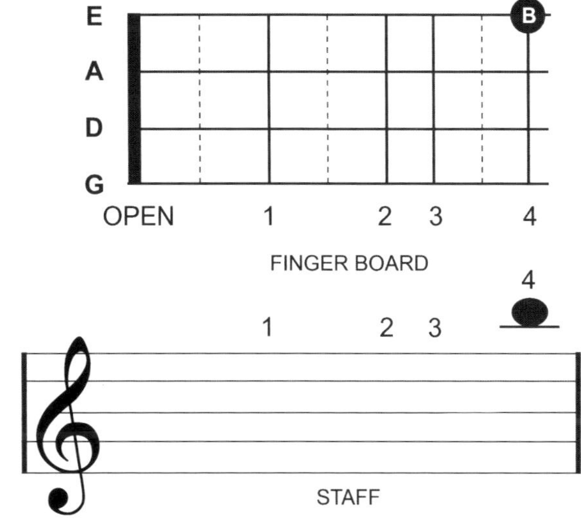

TRACK 34

TURKEY in the STRAW

Use your 4th finger for A in the first full bar, to keep that note group on the D string. Then you will also have two new notes on the G string:

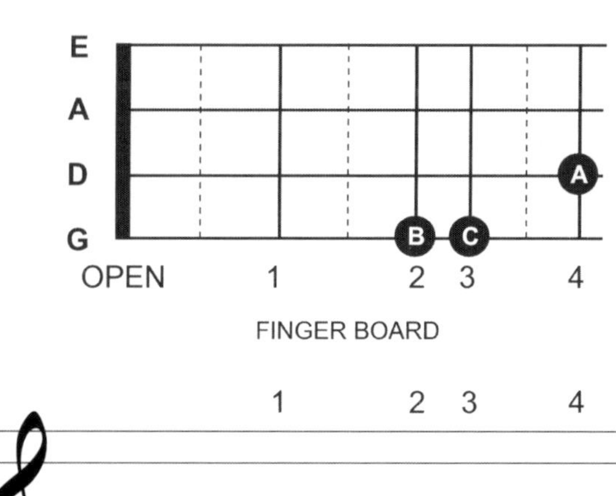

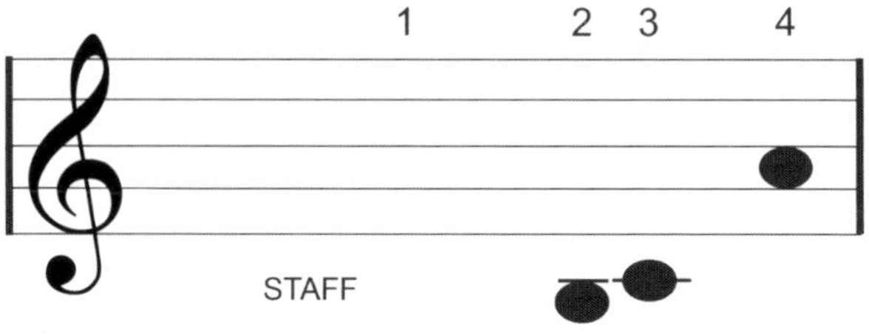

Play the notes with dots above or below them *staccato* (short).

Lift the bow on the endings to allow the final note to ring.

TRACK 35

LOG CHAIN

The three-note slurs tied over the beat, alternating with single down bows, creates the *Georgia* shuffle bowing. **Pull** those down bows extra fast to create a backbeat accent and to equalize the bow strokes.

Section A contains 1st and 3rd finger *double stops* (two notes fingered together) in bars 2, 4 and 6. Leave the 3rd finger down when you play the preceding note, then just add the 1st.

A

D G A7

D G

A7 D 1. D 2.

B

G A7 G

A7 G A7

D A7 D 1. D 2.

BATTLE of NEW ORLEANS

This tune helps you get used to playing extended passages on the G string. Be sure to raise your right arm (keeping that shoulder low and relaxed) to cross over to that string. Likewise, bring your left elbow to the right, well underneath the fiddle, to place your fingers directly over the string.

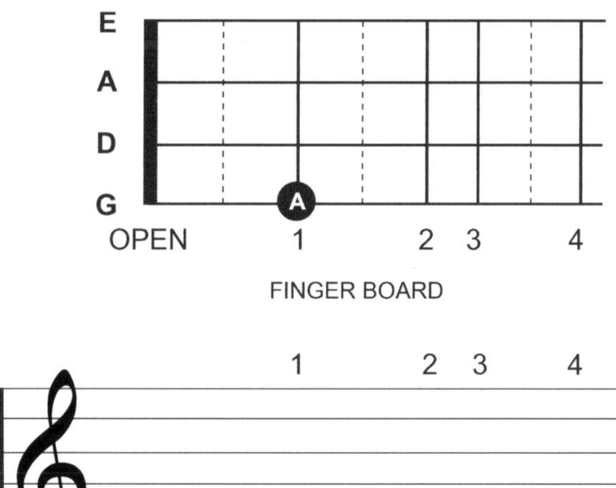

Here's 1st finger (A) on the G string:

A G C D7 G 1. G 2.

B G D7 G

TRACK 38

TENNESSEE WALTZ

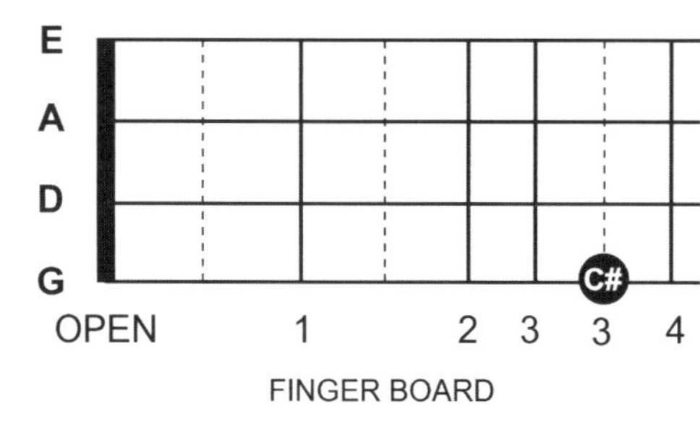

This song is a waltz, in 3/4 time (three beats per measure).

Reach way underneath the fiddle (to the right) with your left elbow to hit this C♯ (high 3rd finger, spaced apart from the 2nd) on the G string:

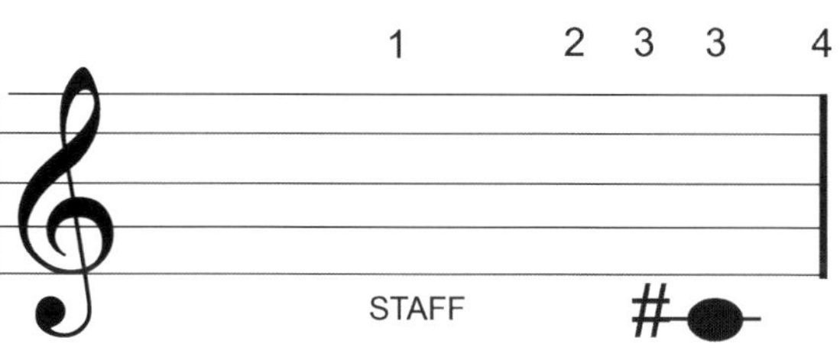

In bars 1 and 2 (and also in the 2nd to last line) you can hold down your 2nd finger to sound the F♯ along with the open A. It's indicated by the line after the 2. (2 ———)

A D D/C♯ D7/C G D D6 1. Em A7 2. A7 D

B D F♯7 G D D6 Em A7 D D/C♯ D7/C G D A7 D

RUBBER DOLLY

Pull the downbow fast on the F♯ slides that start the first three phrases, to emphasize them and equalize the bowstrokes. Conserve your bow on the long tied (same pitches slurred together) notes.

The dashes over the notes ( ) on the 2nd ending of Section A indicate to articulate them with a little extra weight and separation.

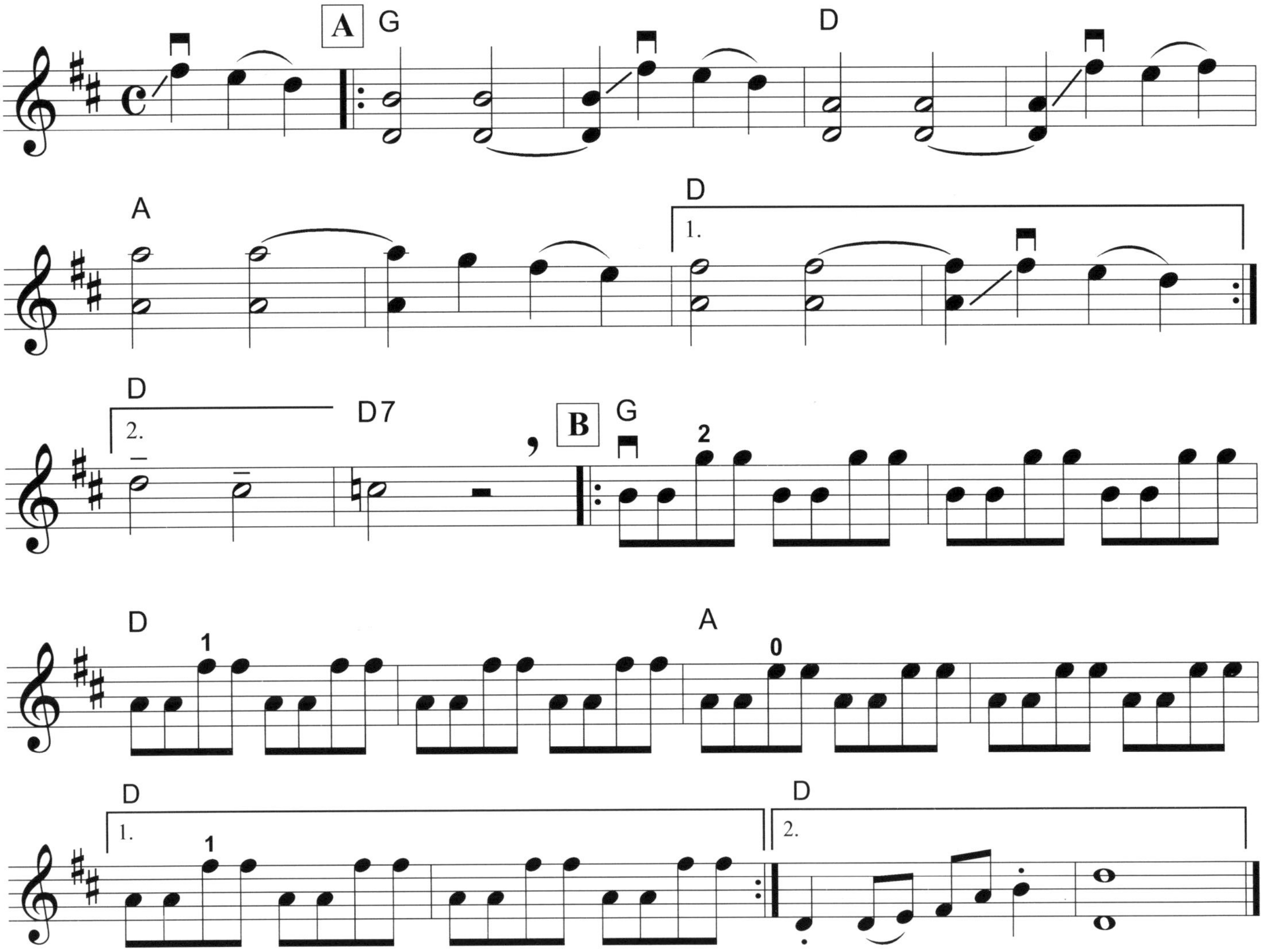

RUBBER DOLLY
ALTERNATE [B] with CROSS-SHUFFLE

We will now substitute *cross-shuffle* bowing (popularized by Erwin T. Rouse in his famous "Orange Blossom Special") in Section B. This 3-note repeated figure superimposed over 4/4 time gives the tune a syncopated feel. Each line contains five sets of 3 with an extra note at the end to total 16 notes. Lift the right elbow quickly to cross over to the D string at the end.

TRACK 40

RUBBER DOLLY
ALTERNATE [B] with ALTERNATING TOP NOTE CROSS-SHUFFLE

For variety, let's shuttle back and forth between two fingers on the top notes now.

RUBBER DOLLY
ALTERNATE [B] with PROGRESSING TOP NOTE CROSS-SHUFFLE

And finally let's make melodic lines with those top notes, going up and down.

RANDOM RAG

Mary Ann Willis

Rags typically have syncopations like the one we just learned.

We also now have *anticipations*, which syncopate by starting a group of four eighth notes one note early, tied over from the previous group (see the middle of bars 2, 3, 4 and 6). Listen to the recording for the timing.

Swing bowing helps give this tune a swing feel.

SALLY GOODIN

This tune also has a swing feel. Its signature is the open A droning in *unison* together with the 4th finger A on the D string in Section A, and the same thing one string higher in Section B. Notice the tied anticipation over bars 5 and 6.

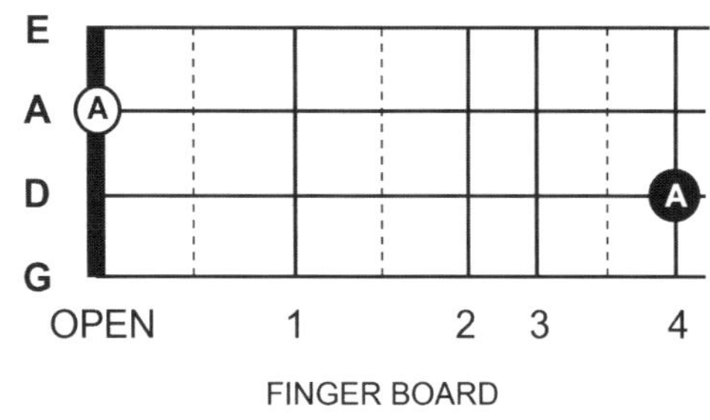

We also have a fast triplet grace note rollup in the second to last bar. 

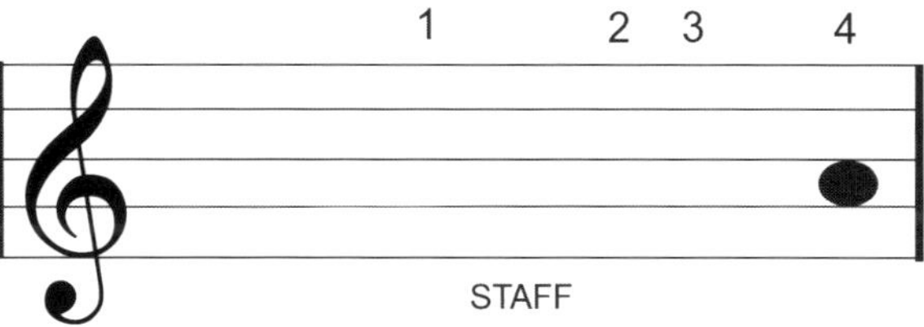

TRACK 44

A

B

BILLY in the LOWGROUND

This tune features a lot of long slurs, a signature of the smooth bluegrass style. It contrasts C major with A *minor* as you can hear in the backup chords.

You will find some identical phrases with different bowings, which will keep things interesting!

TRACK 45

LIBERTY

For the intro *chops*, play consecutive quick downbows, making circles with your right arm to retake the bow each time.

Bars 2 and 4 of Section A begin with *grace notes*. Play these very quickly, before the beat.

TRACK 46

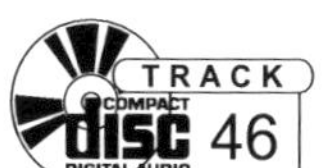

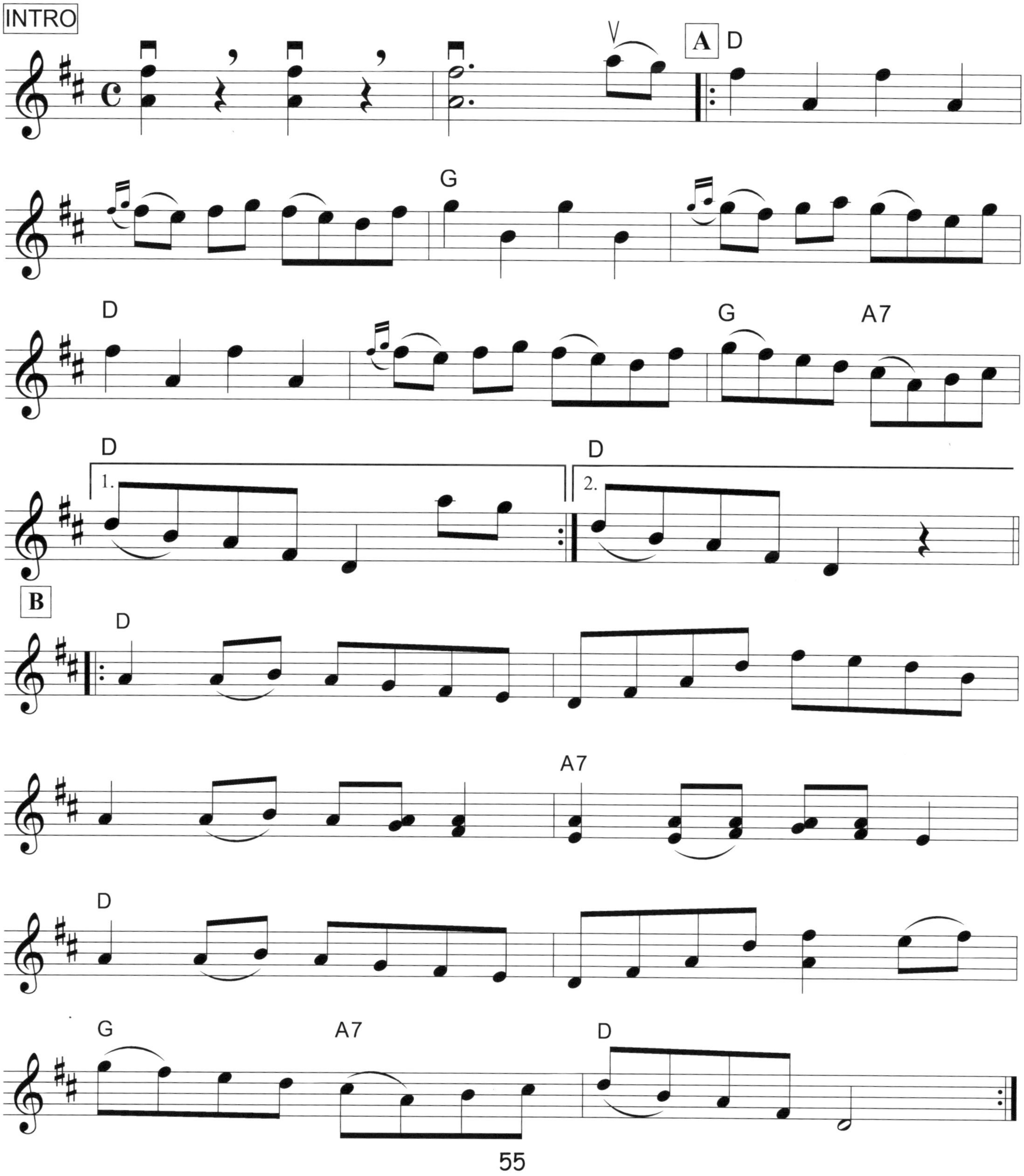
INTRO
A
D
G
D
G
A7
D
1.
D
2.
B
D
A7
D
G
A7
D

I DON'T LOVE NOBODY

We have a blue note E♭ — low 4th finger (touching the 3rd), in addition to the normal E naturals.

You can do a *jazz trill* in bar 8 by rocking your left hand back and forth to periodically strike your 3rd finger while keeping the 2nd down.

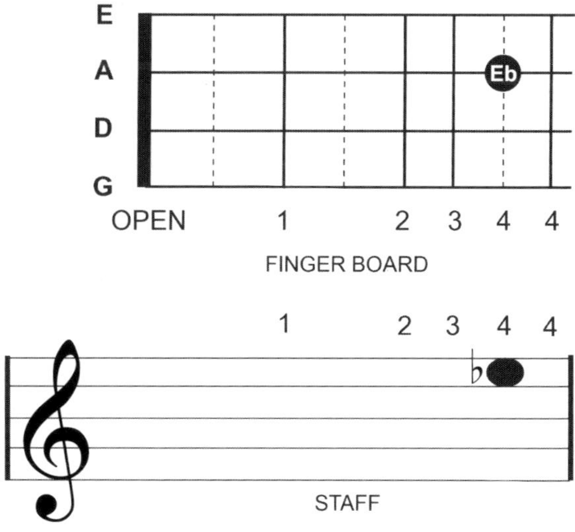

TRACK 47

MARY ANN WILLIS

Mary Ann Willis has taught and performed professionally in Houston, TX since 1977, showcasing eclectic and innovative violin styles. Her audiences range from festival crowds to celebrities and nobility. Her passion is sharing the violin's infinite capabilities of expression.

She has performed

2000-present with Houston's world fusion band Moodafaruka

1979-1999 with Houston's multi-ethnic society band The Gypsies

1976-1977 with the Spoleto, Italy Opera Festival orchestra, and numerous symphony orchestras throughout the United States prior to that.

Mary Ann wrote the book on violin - literally. She is best-selling author of a dozen Gypsy, classical, ethnic, fiddle and technical book/recordings for music instructional world leader Mel Bay Publications as well as various articles for Strings, Strad, and American String Teacher magazines.

She has presented numerous workshops for the American String Teachers Association, Rocky Mountain Fiddle Camp and Strings without Boundaries.

She teaches at Writers in the Round, a music studio dedicated to developing each student's unique talents and style. She has also taught at Houston Community College as well as in her own private studio.

Education and Background

Finishing studies: L'Institut des Hautes Études Musicales, Montreux, Switzerland

California and Texas music teaching credentials

B.A. in classical violin, University of California at Santa Cruz

Also attended Bennington College and San Francisco Conservatory of Music

Mary Ann has studied with native folk violinists and fiddlers and has transcribed and studied repertoire in Hungarian Gypsy, Romanian, Klezmer, Ukrainian, Russian, Polish, Czech, Balkan, Greek, Scandinavian, Mexican, Argentinian, Brasilian, Irish, Scottish, French Canadian, Cape Breton, Northumbrian, Shetland, Texas Contest, Old Time, New England, Bluegrass, and Cajun styles.

PRACTICE TIPS

Practice as often as you can, in short increments.

Tune the fiddle each time.

Listen to a tune before you play it so you know how it goes.

Pluck the notes first to learn them.

For a good tone, maintain good bow position, angle, speed, and pressure (see page 8). Let your ear be your guide.

Use a mirror (holding the fiddle sideways to it) to check your bow angle. Also check your posture and left hand position.

Position your fingers directly over the strings to hit the notes in tune.

Practice the hard parts, gradually working up speed until you can play them as fast as the easy parts.

Listen to and watch other players.

Network and play with other musicians.

Re-visit old tunes to keep them under your fingers.

Record yourself.

Be patient. Good muscle memory takes time to develop!

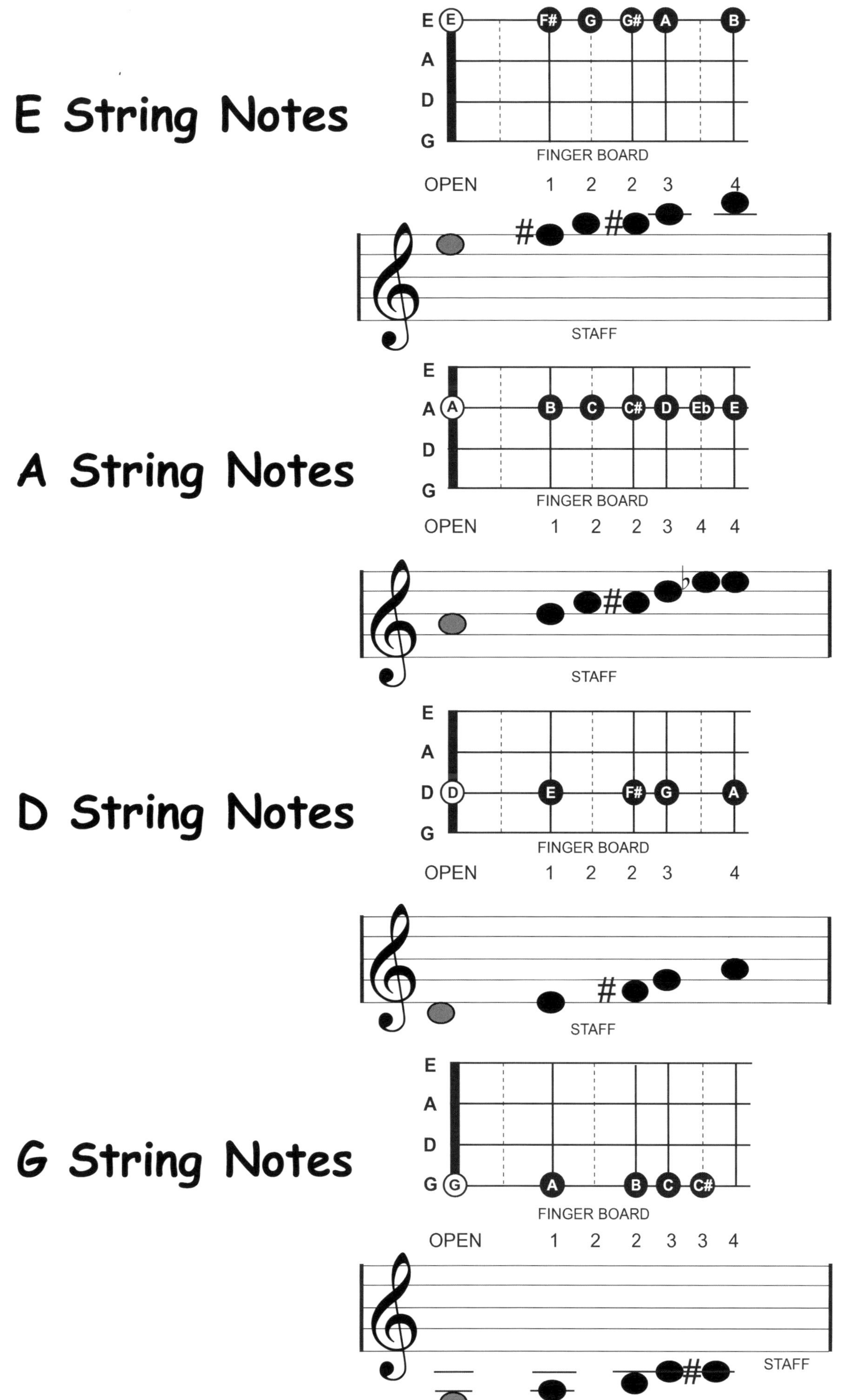
E String Notes
E A D G
E F# G G# A B
FINGER BOARD
OPEN 1 2 2 3 4
STAFF
A String Notes
E A D G
A B C C# D Eb E
FINGER BOARD
OPEN 1 2 2 3 4 4
STAFF
D String Notes
E A D G
D E F# G A
FINGER BOARD
OPEN 1 2 2 3 4
STAFF
G String Notes
E A D G
G A B C C#
FINGER BOARD
OPEN 1 2 2 3 3 4
STAFF

ALPHABETICAL INDEX of TUNES

Angeline the Baker 23

Arkansas Traveler 42

Battle of New Orleans 46

Billy in the Lowground 54

Boil the Cabbage Down 18

Cripple Creek 24

Devil's Dream 40

Hot Cross Buns! 16

I Don't Love Nobody 56

Liberty 55

Liza Jane 30

Log Chain 45

Mary Had a Little Lamb 22

McNab's Hornpipe 28

Old Joe Clark 31

Pop! Goes the Weasel 36

Random Rag 52

Red-Haired Boy 35

Rubber Dolly 48

Sally Goodin 53

Soldier's Joy 36

St. Anne's Reel 43

Tennessee Waltz 47

Turkey in the Straw 44